A Biblical Counselor's Approach to Marital Abuse:
Roadmap to Reunification

Completely Revised and Updated!

by
Julie Ganschow & Bill Schlacks

A Biblical Counselor's Approach to Marital Abuse:
Roadmap to Reunification

Copyright © 2018 by Julie Ganschow and Bill Schlacks
Second Edition, November 2020
Cover Artwork by Andrea Loy Designs

All "counselee" representations are fictitious and do not represent anyone living or dead or their actual case histories or personal stories.

Library of Congress Control Number:
ISBN- 978-0-578-81056-0
Published by *Pure Water Press* - Kansas City, MO
Printed in the United States of America.

Table of Contents

Preface

This book addresses the topic of domestic abuse, domestic violence, and oppression in marriage. Throughout this book, we use those terms as well as "abuse," "abuser," and "victim." We understand "domestic abuse" is a secular construct and that these terms come with baggage. We recognize that our readers are probably very familiar with them and understand the secular framework for those terms related to this book's topic. We do not use these terms indiscriminately, and we do not always agree with their secular understanding.

Why use secular terminology when we know you are looking for a biblical perspective on this topic? Well, we use them for ease in addressing the subject. We expose the worldly baggage that goes along with them and then seek to teach you, our readers, how to approach those terms/issues/concepts biblically and think about them rightly.

At its foundation, domestic abuse and oppression is sin. Sin is no respecter of persons; therefore, either a man or woman can be an abuser. Women are equally capable of being emotionally, physically, verbally, spiritually, and even sexually abusive. However, the clear majority of those coming to our counseling center are women who are being abused by men. For this reason, when not otherwise identified, the abuser will be portrayed as a male, and the victim will be represented as a female.

If you have been affected by domestic abuse and have picked up this book looking for help, please understand that the *Roadmap* is not intended to be followed as a prescriptive, hard-and-fast methodology. We think it is necessary to say this because, in the years since we wrote the original version of this book, we have had victims of abuse say, "But in your book, you say (blank) should happen next!" People are not predictable, and your situation comes with individual personalities and complexities. We would not presume to tell you a hard and fast, step by step method to reconciling your marriage. Those following our *Roadmap* should understand that the journey often encounters detours, delays, and unexpected obstacles. This is one aspect of the sanctification process and cannot be forced or rushed.

If you desire to help those affected by domestic violence or oppression, we have presented you with an updated *Roadmap* to counsel them biblically. As we indicated in the first version of this book, this is an ongoing project. Even in this second edition, we recognize that we have not addressed every possible issue or scenario. We plan to continue to refine and add to this material to provide the most up to date information to help pastors and biblical counselors serve the men and women affected by domestic abuse and violence.

Our *Roadmap* is not a concrete plan, nor should it be considered as a "method" or something applicable in every situation. As a biblical counselor, you know that the counseling situations you will encounter are unique. Our goal in this updated version of this book was to offer a more balanced approach and share the things we have learned along the way.

The biblical counselor is expected to use their own sound wisdom and discernment when providing services to those in need. Our counseling team has benefited from the knowledge of those who have produced and written excellent materials on this subject. However, the inclusion of quotations found in this book does not mean we fully endorse or recommend their approach to abuse counseling.

As with all materials, we suggest you read and process the contents with wisdom and discernment. Please read the introduction before moving into the rest of the book.

Introduction

Reports and concerns about domestic violence have surged to the forefront in our communities and our churches. Our research indicates that the prevalence of domestic violence is the same *in the church* as in the secular world. The requests for biblical counseling through our counseling center have continued to increase since we wrote the first edition of this book in September 2018. Many of those who are seeking our help cite "marital issues," "conflict," or "the need for marital counseling" on their intake paperwork. Astonishingly, a significant number of that group of counselees are abusers or victims of abuse.

At Reigning Grace Counseling Center, we receive referrals for couples where domestic abuse is suspected from churches in and around the greater Kansas City area. We also welcome referrals from those scouring the internet looking for information and resources, as well as from our online presence with the Association of Certified Biblical Counselors (ACBC), the International Association of Biblical Counselors (IABC), and our website (www.rgcconline.org), which brings us counselees from all over the world.

We prefer to meet face-to-face with our counselees whenever possible. However, in this cyberage, internet applications such as Zoom Video Conferencing, Skype, and

FaceTime all increase our ability to reach those looking for help who are many miles away.

I (Julie) am a biblical counselor who primarily ministers to women. When my counselee is the victim of domestic abuse, I help her understand oppression and abuse (what has happened) biblically and walk with her through the counseling process. I also work with women who abuse their husbands. I (Bill) work with the men, who are most frequently the abusers. I help them understand the role their hearts play in abuse or oppression and then direct them to what the Bible says are ways of glorifying God by how they relate to their wives.

Our purpose for writing this book is to present a *Roadmap to Reunification* for counselors helping people affected by domestic abuse and oppression. We provide biblical counsel on recognizing abuse, repentance of sin at the heart level (sanctification), reconciliation of the couple, and, whenever possible, the reunification of the family. However, our counseling goal is not ultimately reunification, but that each counselee would begin to glorify God by how they live their lives.

The Roadmap looks like this:

Recognition - You Are Here. Before starting on any journey, the counselees must know where they are in relation to where they are going. Some things to think about before beginning a journey are how long it will take to get there, what will be needed along the way, and who will accompany the counselees on their journey. This beginning point of the journey emphasizes the need for both the abuser and the victim to understand that what has been taking place in their relationship is abusive in nature and limits and diminishes another person as an image-bearer of God.

Repentance - One Way Forward. Repentance is the only way forward in a marriage that has been affected by abuse. We recommend meeting separately with the victim and the abuser, counseling each of them toward repenting of their ungodly heart attitudes and behaviors.

The abuser must admit and recognize they have sinned without blame-shifting, rationalization, or justification. Most importantly, they are to experience a change of heart about their sin (repentance). As a result, they no longer desire to demonstrate ungodly coercive power, control, and anger in their life, and they begin to address the sins of the heart. The victim also repents of the sinful thoughts, beliefs, and desires that have developed in their heart as responses to mistreatment.

Reconciliation - Navigating New Roads. Couples that have struggled with domestic abuse will navigate new roads individually and together in the process of reconciliation. *The Roadmap* includes the abuser making a full disclosure and the spouse responding with how the abuse has affected them. As counseling progresses, the couple will engage in conflict resolution, learn biblical communication, have supervised interactions, supervised dating, and couples' counseling.

Reunification - Charting A New Course. At this point in the journey, the couple begins to chart a new course forward. They will engage in phone calls, continue dating with less supervision, have home visits, and re-engage in family life until they are gradually reunited. The counseling team has decreasing involvement as the family is returned to the local church's full care.

Don't be fooled by the apparent simplicity of *The Roadmap*--there is a significant amount of counseling that takes place in each of these phases. Depending on the severity of the abusive treatment and the willingness to repent and change, the journey can take many months or even years.

Recognition

You Are Here

Most of us are probably familiar with large maps that have an arrow pointing to a specific spot on the map with the words, "You are here." Knowing where you are on a map helps orient you as to where you are in relation to where you want to go.

This point on the *Roadmap* will orient the counselor in helping each person recognize what they are doing and experiencing to move forward.

What Is Abuse?

There is no doubt that the Bible recognizes physical, emotional, and verbal abuse; it just uses different terminology that reflects biblical anthropology. Few people dispute the reality of physical abuse. However, because emotional and verbal abuse is not as clear cut, they are often diminished or discounted altogether.

A succinct definition of abuse is elusive as "abuse" is multifaceted. To provide you with a broad spectrum of understanding, we have gathered several commonly accepted meanings of abuse types from various sources. A dictionary definition of abuse is,

> Improperly or excessively using or misusing someone. Hurting or injuring them by maltreatment, rough treatment, physical violence. Abuse is also forced or coerced sexual activity, insulting, reviling or hurtful

language when used to threaten or demoralize another person.[1]

Biblical counselor Sherry Allchin defines abuse as, "To wrongly or improperly misuse. To hurt or injure by maltreatment, contemptuous, coarse, insulting words, angry reactions (Col. 3:8; Eph. 4:29-31).[2]

Pastor Chris Moles defines domestic violence this way,

> A pattern of abusive behavior in any relationship that is used by one partner to gain or maintain power and control over another intimate partner. Domestic violence can be physical, sexual, emotional, economic, or psychological actions or threats of actions that influence another person. This includes any behaviors that intimidate, manipulate, humiliate, isolate, frighten, terrorize, coerce, threaten, blame, hurt, injure, or wound someone.[3]

When we at Reigning Grace use the term "abuse," this is what we mean: Abuse is habitual, excessive, and destructive patterns of sinful behavior that exert coercive power and control over another person. These behaviors use or hurt another person physically, sexually, or emotionally without regard for how the actions affect the recipient. Abusive behaviors instill fear (fear of being hurt, fear of exposure,

---

[1] Farlex. (2018, 8 9). *The Free Dictionary.* www.thefreedictionary.com:https://www.thefreedictionary.com/abusing

[2] Sherry Allchin, *Helping Women Who Have Experienced Domestic Violence,* workshop presented at the 2018 ACBC Annual Conference, *Light In the Darkness.*

[3] Chris Moles, *The Heart of Domestic Abuse,* Module One: *The Extent of the Problem,* Lesson One: *Domestic Violence in the Christian Home: What is Domestic Violence?* PeaceWorks University Live Online Course, August 2019.

fear of not being believed) and break the recipient down physically and emotionally and confuse them to the point they think they are crazy.

Who is the Abuser?

Abuse is not new. However, there has been an intense focus on abuse and its effects over the past ten years. Both male and female victims are coming forward with stories of abuse in their homes. Statistics reveal that "1 in 4 women (24.3%) and 1 in 7 men (13.8%) aged 18 and older in the United States have been the victim of severe physical violence by an intimate partner in their lifetime."[4]

Nearly half of all women and men in the United States have experienced psychological aggression by an intimate partner in their lifetime.[5] This statistic is important to note. While non-physical abuse is typically considered to be primarily male on female, statistically, women are increasingly perpetrating acts of domestic oppression and emotional and verbal abuse against men.[6]

Domestic Abuse and Mental Illness

According to the National Domestic Violence Hotline, it is commonly assumed that those who abuse others have a "mental illness" that causes them to abuse. Still, current secular thinking is that this is not true. Often, victims who

---

[4] National Domestic Violence Hotline, General, https://www.thehotline.org/resources/statistics/, accessed 5-30-2020

[5] Ibid.

[6] Donald Dutton, Tonia L. Nicholls Tonia, Alicia Spidel, *Female Perpetrators of Intimate Abuse*, in Women Who Perpetrate Relationship Violence: Moving Beyond Political Correctness, The Haworth Press, Inc., http://www.haworthpress.com/web/JOR 2005, p 1-6.

are desperate to explain or understand why their husbands or wives hurt them tell us their spouse has been diagnosed with bipolar disorder, depression, anxiety, post-traumatic stress disorder (PTSD), borderline personality, or antisocial personality disorder.[7]

We work with the counselee to understand these behaviors and the terminology through a biblical lens. As biblical counselors, we do not deny the existence of genuine medical disease or illness. However, there is too much that is unknown about the etiology of the behaviors that lead to such diagnoses in the realm of mental health.[8]

We will attempt not to take you too far into the weeds. Still, we believe a basic understanding of what undergirds these diagnoses and the terminology is crucial to how you, as a biblical counselor, will approach helping a victim or perpetrator of domestic abuse. Your epistemology (a presuppositional belief that underlies all claims of truth and knowledge) and your anthropological view of man (the study of the human and human life related to God)[9] are critically important in helping a person overcome any problem. This especially true when counseling domestic abuse.

There are foundational evolutionary beliefs and mental illness theories that have established what is known as the brain dysfunction theory, which has evolved into what is today called "mental illness." Mental illnesses are

---

[7] https://www.thehotline.org/2015/05/06/abuse-and-mental-illness-is-there-a-connection/

[8] We highly recommend the books written by Dr. Daniel Berger II for an in-depth look at Mental Illness and its foundations.

[9] Christian Anthropology, Wikkipedia, https://en.wikipedia.org/wiki/Christian_anthropology, accessed 6/7/2020

considered diseases of the mind, according to the DSM-5. Secular therapists and even some Christian integrative counselors (unwittingly, we hope) believe the mind is a *material object and that the mind's operations are considered* aspects of the brain (the Materialist view of man).

Christians who accept psychological pseudoscience are inviting deceptive and destructive philosophies and traditions of human wisdom to override biblical discernment. We who profess a belief in the Bible cannot righteously accept secular answers about man or his problems. Furthermore, we cannot accept pseudoscientific solutions to those problems. God's Word reveals why it is not wisdom but pure foolishness to look to secular sources or embrace secular methodologies to help those suffering in a domestic violence situation. Isaiah 55:8-9 says, *"For My thoughts are not your thoughts, nor are your ways My ways," declares the LORD. "For as the heavens are higher than the earth, so are My ways higher than your ways And My thoughts than your thoughts."*

We agree with John MacArthur, who says,

> "I have no quarrel with those who use either common sense or social sciences as a helpful observer's platform to look on human conduct and develop tools to assist people in getting some external controls in their behavior. That may be useful as a first step for getting to the real spiritual cure. But a wise counselor realizes that all behavioral therapy stops on the surface, far short of actual solutions to the real needs of the soul, which are resolved only in Christ. On the other hand, I have no tolerance for those who exalt psychology above Scripture, intercession, and the perfect sufficiency of our God. And I have no encouragement for people who wish

to mix psychology with the divine resources and sell the mixture as a spiritual elixir. Their methodology amounts to a tacit admission that what God has given us in Christ is not really adequate to meet our deepest needs and salve our troubled lives." [10]

For our purposes, we will define such behaviors biblically. What secularists and integrationists consider various disorders of the material mind/brain, the Bible declares to be spiritual in nature and products of the deliberate choices of the sinful heart that includes the mind. There is no evidence that a brain illness ever caused someone to act contrary to God's moral will.

Like Pharisees

Our philosophy of ministry at Reigning Grace is "Heart Change for Life Change." The abusive person, and frequently, the person they hurt, will often attempt to blame something exterior such as their upbringing for their abusive behaviors. No one wants to believe such words and deeds can flow from within another person, but Scripture says otherwise (Mk. 7:14-24).

> Abusive men come from every walk of life, every income bracket, and every race and culture. With rare exceptions, friends, family, and business associates never guess or suspect wife abuse by the abuser's behavior in their presence. [11]

---

[10] John MacArthur, *Counseling: How to Counsel Biblically*, (Nashville: Thomas Nelson, Inc., 2005), 16.

[11] Debi Pryde, & Robert Needham, *A Biblical Perspective of What to do When You Are Abused by Your Husband*, 16.

As unfortunate as this truth is, it is no surprise to God; He does not overlook it and, as he says in Psalm 11:4-5, *"Those who love violence he hates with a passion."* As a biblical counselor, one must understand that God hates violence against his people and does not overlook the abuse. Those who abuse others twist theology and are deceived in their thinking about sin.

The metaphor of the wolf in sheep's clothing is appropriate here. This metaphor is used to describe false prophets throughout the Bible, but it is also true of those who are pharisaical. We have repeatedly encountered abusive people who look like Christians. They are sometimes involved in ministry, respected among their church members. The public face is dramatically different from the private face that the abuser's spouse and children see at home. We are faced with someone whose public profession of faith does not privately line up with the life/actions of a Christian, except that they read the Bible (often faithfully), attend, and or serve in church or ministry. Their public persona is that of a Christian, and by all outward appearances, they are what they say they are or profess to be. Privately, however, they are very different people, and in the counseling process, they are further revealed to be unwilling or unable to repent and change. It seems they are filled with head knowledge about God and His Word but are unable or are blind to how their abusive sinful behavior conflicts with their profession and stated beliefs. Their sin is habitual, not occasional. It is a lifestyle, not an incident or an episode. We see them as self-deceived people who are unable or unwilling to comprehend how their sinful abusive tactics of abuse directly conflict with the gospel and the imperatives of Scripture. We could consider some of those who sinfully abuse their spouses as modern-day Pharisees.

The Pharisees of Jesus' day were men who devoted their lives to studying Scripture. They were very attentive to the Law's letter and held others accountable to it but did not adhere to it themselves. They lived, "Don't do as I do, do as I say" (Matt. 23:3-4). As you will see in the section, *Tactics Used to Gain and Maintain Power and Control*, those who sinfully abuse their spouse will demonstrate the conflict between what they say they believe and the reality of how they live. They construct systems of behavior and practices that consist of personal preferences not found in Scripture to hide what is really going on in their heart. Worse yet, they will be unable to let go of their tactics because this would expose them as the hypocrites they are. They are very devoted to covering their sin instead of repenting of their sin (Matt. 23:25-28).

Those who sin by abusing their spouse frequently use the Scriptures to "leverage" or manipulate their spouse into seeing things their way. This includes the victim seeing themselves through the eyes of their abuser. The spouse will use Ephesians 5:22-23 or 1 Peter 3:1-6 to point out their "failures." This type of Pharisee is like the priest who walked past the beaten man dying in the road (Luke 10:31-32). They have no compassion for their spouse and are invested in living for themselves.

Another commonality between the abusive person and the Pharisees is they practice righteousness to be seen by others (Matt. 6:5). Jesus condemned the Pharisees for their hypocrisy. They pretended to be godly men, examples for others to follow. They knew all the right things to say in public, to look and sound like godly examples to be followed. Such people love to argue about how they are "right" and are adept at pointing out their spouse's flaws.

However, they are blind to their own sin (Matt. 7:3-5). Jesus called them hypocrites in Matthew 15:7-8, *"You hypocrites, rightly did Isaiah prophesy of you: 'This people honors Me with their lips, but their heart is far away from Me."*

The Pharisee presents a unique challenge and difficulty to the biblical counselor. The question is one of genuine conversion. When we are faced with a person who cannot or will not change, can or should we continue to believe they are a Christian? The biblical counselor recognizes their counselee's standing with God is more important than their status with their spouse. This behavior and situation are a gift to allow the counselors to help them with behavior that may indicate their standing or relationship with God.

We must not be afraid to challenge our counselees' conversion when there is little evidence to verify their profession of faith. Consider we may be doing them a disservice by being too timid to confront their lack of repentance and change as an indication they are dead in their sin (Eph. 2:1).

Often, such people have prominent roles in the church or serve in various capacities (i.e., deacon, teacher, women's ministry leader, elder, usher, worship team). We recommend to the pastors we work with that they consider temporarily removing both the husband and wife from church service. This is not punitive; it communicates the gravity of the situation and allows the couple to focus on their relationship with God and fully participate in the counseling process.

The Heart of Pride

"Pride and arrogance are surely at work within the heart of an abusive man."[12] The primary root of domestic abuse is pride. The abuser's heart is focused on themselves. Their violent or oppressive actions result from the thoughts, beliefs, and desires of their heart.

Both the victim and the abuser must understand that the abuser is being deceived by their sinful heart (Jer. 17:9). Because the heart of man is deceptive and desperately wicked, it is beyond their ability to understand it. Their heart is lying to them all the time.

One of our counseling goals is for the victim to understand that their abuser's heart is so effective at lying that often, the perpetrator does not realize that their rationalizations and justifications of their abusive actions are sinful. Furthermore, because the heart's thoughts are desperately wicked (Gen. 6:5), they should not be surprised that their abuser acts as they do. Instead, we should be grateful that things are not worse, no matter how bad it is presently.

Chris Moles says, "The prideful man seeks his own benefit and looks to gain praise and support."[13] The abuser is arrogant and concerned with being "the king of the castle." The willingness to abuse is evidence that they will do anything to obtain and maintain that position. They do not concern themselves with God's glory but instead seek to

---

[12] Chris Moles, *The Heart of Domestic Abuse: Gospel Solutions for Men Who Use Control and Violence in the Home,* 44.

[13] Ibid. 44.

establish themselves as a god to their spouse and children. They seek to be in control of their household and to be the center of attention. They cannot tolerate others in their home receiving recognition, adoration, attention, or approval.

> They [abusers] lust for the adoration of others (dare we say worship), living for the accolades and praises of those around them, yet knowing in their hearts that they are undeserving of such honors.[14]

Narcissism

Those who commit acts of violence against their intimate partner or spouse are often labeled as "narcissists" by other domestic violence care providers. Narcissistic Personality Disorder is a DSM-5 diagnosis, that according to the MayoClinic Online, is "a disorder in which a person has an inflated sense of self-importance. Narcissistic Personality Disorder is found more commonly in men. The cause is unknown but likely involves a combination of genetic and environmental factors."[15]

Some people teach that a narcissist cannot change, but this is not true. Here again, we find the materialist view that essentially removes personal responsibility for such ungodly behaviors from the person committing them. It is not their fault; it is their genes or how they were raised.

"While the descriptions are similar between the secular and Biblical world, God does not view "narcissism" as a

---

[14] Warren Lamb, *Behind the Veil; Exposing he Evil of Domestic Oppression and Providing Hope,* Self-published, 2019, 17.

[15] https://www.mayoclinic.org/diseases-conditions/narcissistic-personality-disorder/symptoms-causes/syc-20366662#:~:text=Overview,lack%20of%20empathy%20for%20others.

mere personality disorder. He sees narcissistic behavior as an evil that is driven by what is in a person's heart."[16] We have been asked if a Christian can struggle with narcissism, and the answer is "yes,"

Though the Bible does not use the word "narcissist," it identifies many of the narcissist's behaviors and motives. Proverbs 21:24 identifies such a person as having "insolent pride," being "proud," "haughty," and a "scoffer."

No one will tell a narcissist what to do; he tells others what to do. They desire to control another person through self-serving (Mk. 7:9-13) and manipulative actions (Jude 16-19). The narcissist creates smokescreens to obscure their self-centered actions (Matt. 23:5-7; Mk. 12:38-44).

Such people are described throughout the Bible, and their behaviors are identified as being haughty (Prov. 21:24), arrogant (Prov. 15:12; Jer. 49:16), deceptive (Ps. 12:2), hypocritical (Matt. 15:7-9), and self-seeking (Deut. 8:11-15). The narcissist excels at making themselves look good on the outside while being rotten on the inside (Matt. 23:25).

Robertsson says,

> Narcissists have a whole different attitude toward conflict. They use it strategically to manipulate. They seek conflict. They become impossible people, flying into conflict with you over anything you think, say, do, feel, or wear. As if THEY have the right to determine what you say, think, do, feel, or wear.[17]

---

[16] DC Robertsson, *The First Will be Last: A Biblical Perspective on Narcissism*, Kindle Edition, Davidson Trust Publishing, 2015, 23.

[17] Ibid. 36.

Because the Bible admonishes Christians to repent of pride (Phil. 2:3-4; Jas. 4:6; 1 Pet. 5:5), the Christian struggling with insolent pride can and must repent and change. All things are possible with God (Matt. 19:26).

Paulo attempts to control Joan's thoughts, words, and actions by using his emotions and verbal tirades to manipulate her. Paulo over talks. He does not have conversations; he performs monologues with people to control the narrative. When Joan attempts to clarify something she has said or done, Paulo refuses to accept her word or explanation. Instead, he insists that his interpretation of her words, meanings, and motives are accurate. He is effective at convincing others he is right and amassing others to support his position.

Paulo believes he is righteous before God and does not hesitate to tell you so repeatedly. To make himself look good, he quotes Scriptures and talks about his positive relationship with God. All the while, he is attacking, blaming, slandering, criticizing, and judging Joan and anyone else who disagrees with his opinions. Ironically, he does not see his hypocrisy and becomes enraged when he is challenged.

Types of Abusive Behavior

There are numerous ways that people abuse each other. We have listed the most common forms of abuse found in domestic and intimate partner relationships. The secular terms "emotional abuse," "verbal abuse," "domestic abuse," and "oppression "are umbrella terms that are loaded with assumptions and implications and can be misunderstood by the general public as well as by Christians. While we should not entirely avoid their usage, we suggest identifying "abusive" behaviors with words found in the Scriptures whenever possible.

Physical Abuse

Physical abuse is directed toward the physical body and includes bullying or threatening actions, assault, and battery (punching, kicking, hitting, breaking bones, slapping, wounding, choking, pushing, shoving, restraining, tripping, or burning. The assault leaves bruises, scratches, burns, welts, and other marks on a person's body, whether or not they are visible. Some abusers will only hit in places covered or hidden by clothing (Ps. 11:5; 13:2; 56:1-2a, 5-6).

Physical abuse is a crime and is punishable by law (Rom. 13:1-4). When physical abuse occurs, the victim should call the police and press charges against the abuser, even if the abuser is her husband or intimate partner.

Sexual Abuse

Sexual abuse is another form of physical abuse. It includes withholding of affection, insisting/demanding, rape, weaponizing sex, manipulating with sex and for sex (scheming), and indifference to her needs, selfish demands (frequency, time of day or night, so-called makeup sex), thoughtlessness/callousness, obsession with sex (bring it up regularly), comparison to other women, judging, mocking, demeaning, and shaming the woman. Sexual abuse includes insisting on or demanding sexual acts and rape (human or object). "Forced sex, even by a spouse or intimate partner with whom you also have consensual sex, is an act of aggression and violence."[18]

---

[18] Justin Holcomb & Lindsay Holcomb, *Is It My Fault? Hope and Healing for Those Suffering Domestic Violence.* (Chicago,Illinois: Moody Publishers, 2014), 36.

Non-Physical Abuse

While attacks on the body can be visible, assaults on the immaterial/non-physical/spiritual part of a person are not readily seen but are equally devastating. These forms of abuse are committed against the victim's emotions and feelings, thoughts, beliefs and desires, soul, and will (Ps. 52:2).

Domestic Oppression

To oppress means one person is subjecting another person to prolonged cruel or unjust treatment.[19] Biblical counselor and Pastor Warren Lamb defined domestic oppression as "An ongoing pattern of intimidating and domineering behavior employed by one family member to control other family members."[20] The oppressor is an "emotional predator" whose goal is to hijack another personhood and break them down on every level.

While domestic oppression is not yet considered an official term for domestic violence, Lamb believes this needs to change. He thinks that domestic oppression is the foundation for every form of abuse. He says,

> Domestic oppressors systematically tyrannize, emotionally coerce, dehumanize, objectify, demean, degrade, manipulate, and bully at least one other person within the family home – usually their spouse – to fuel their idolatry of power and control. It rarely stops there but is then perpetrated on the entire household.[21]

---

[19] "Oppression," Lexico Online Dictionary, https://www.lexico.com/en/definition/oppression, accessed 5/30/2020.

[20] Warren Lamb, *Behind the Veil, 11.*

[21] Ibid. 12.

Emotional and Verbal Abuse

Similar to domestic oppression is emotional abuse. Emotional and verbal abuse almost always go together. These forms of abuse are much more subtle than physical abuse, but they are *still considered abuse.* The person who is being verbally and emotionally abused will not have physical bruises or identifying marks on their body, but this does not mean they are not being harmed by what is taking place in the relationship.

This form of abuse is daily, constant, and long-term, and often the person does not realize that "abuse" is taking place. "Verbal abuse" is biblically defined as sinful speech that is hurtful, demeaning and destructive, as language that tears another person down (Eph. 4:29; Prov. 12:13a; 10:11; 16:27), is cruel (Prov.27:4a), explosive (Prov. 29:22; 15:18), hateful (Prov. 26:24-28; 1 John 4:20; 3:15; 2:9), extremely critical (Gal. 5:15; Jas. 2:13), attacking (Ps. 56:1-2, 55:3) threatening (Ps. 94:4; 83:2; 10:7), harsh (1 Sam. 25:3; Job 30:21, blame-shifting (Prov. 19:3; 28:13), deceptive (Eph. 4:25), contains angry and bitter words (Eph. 4:31), is slanderous and gossipy (Prov. 11:13; 16:28; Ps. 101:5; Prov. 10:18), and malicious (Prov. 26:24-26).

Justin and Lindsay Holcomb add to our understanding:

> Isolation, intimidation and controlling behavior are also signs of emotional abuse. Sometimes abusers throw in threats of physical violence (to the woman or someone she cares about) or other repercussions if you don't do what they want... Emotional abuse can include *economic abuse* such as withholding money and necessities,

restricting you to an allowance, sabotaging your job, and stealing from you or taking your money.[22]

Joy Forrest, herself a survivor of domestic violence, says that in emotional abuse,

> Victims are made to feel like they are constantly wrong, incompetent, and worthless. No matter what the issue, and no matter who is right or wrong, everything gets turned around, and the victim ends up getting blamed for everything.[23]

Often the behaviors have become such a part of everyday life that they do not understand or realize they are being abused, especially when there is no physical evidence of the treatment. Some people live in an emotionally and verbally abusive or oppressive relationship for years or decades without ever experiencing physical harm. The abuser may have smashed and broken items in the home, punched holes in the walls, or displayed anger in other ways, but may not have touched them. It is essential to understand that when someone lives under the threat of violence, there is often no need for the more powerful person actually to lay a hand on them. The threat that they *could be violent* is enough to keep the oppressed person in line.

Abuse is kinetic; that is, it is always changing and progressing. For example, the Holcomb's say, "Verbal abuse is one of the biggest indicators that physical abuse may follow."[24] For this reason, it is wise always to consider a

---

[22] Justin Holcomb & Lindsay Holcomb, *Is It My Fault?* 37.

[23] Joy Forrest, *Called to Peace: A Survivor's Guide to Finding Peace and Healing After Domestic Abuse.* (Raleigh, NC: Blue Ink Press. 2018), 78.

[24] Justin Holcomb & Lindsay Holcomb, *Is It My Fault?* 65.

verbally and emotionally abused person to be in danger of becoming a physically abused person.

Those who abuse are incredibly manipulative (as demonstrated in Luke 10:40) and are driven by a desire to dominate and control others (self-sovereignty).[25] Aspects of abusive and oppressive behavior can be found in what Paul says will characterize people in the last days:

> *For people will be lovers of self, lovers of money, proud, arrogant, abusive, disobedient to their parents, ungrateful, unholy, heartless, unappeasable, slanderous, without self-control, brutal, not loving good, treacherous, reckless, swollen with conceit, lovers of pleasure rather than lovers of God, having the appearance of godliness, but denying its power.* 2 Timothy 3:1-5 (ESV)

The Bible describes the effects on a person who lives in an abusive relationship as suffering from a "broken spirit" (Prov. 15:13), having "pain of heart" (Isa. 65:14), being "crushed in spirit" (Ps. 34:18), or being "broken-hearted" (Ps. 34:18). One of the most devastating features of this kind of treatment is how it chips away at how people view themselves. Their identity as a person of value and worth, created in the image and likeness of God (Gen. 1:26), is diminished as they come to believe what the abuser says about them is true rather than what God in His Word says about them.

A biblical understanding of abuse provides us with a biblical framework for helping both the victim and perpetrator of what is considered to be domestic abuse and

---

[25] Keith Palmer, *Sword Words: Biblical Counseling & Verbal Abuse,* Grace Bible Church, The Center for Biblical Counseling and Discipleship (CBCD), 2018.

oppression. When we at Reigning Grace use the terms "emotional and verbal abuse" or "oppression," we refer to them through the biblical understanding of such actions, words, and behaviors.

Because the Bible identifies the actions of abuse and recognizes the effects of being abused, we can trust it is sufficient to provide help, healing, and hope for both the victim and perpetrator of abuse.

How Do I Know It's Abuse?

The counselor must take all claims of abuse seriously. The counselee will be watching you (the counselor) very carefully to gauge your reaction and responses to what they tell you about their marriage and home life. Rick Thomas says that when a woman confides abuse to someone, "**even the hint of doubt** (that you believe her) can throw the abused person into an emotional tailspin. The one thing that she needs more than anything else is for someone to believe her."[26] As Christians and biblical counselors, we have an obligation to protect victims of abuse and ensure their safety (Ps. 82:3-4; 10:17-18; Prov. 31:8-9, 22:22-23; Jn. 8:59, 10:39; Acts 9:25). We also have a responsibility to protect someone from being falsely accused.

We recognize that marriages have ups and downs, good times and bad and that two sinners living in a home together will struggle mightily at times. Everyone can demonstrate ungodly, selfish, and cruel behaviors from time to time.

---

[26] Rick Thomas, *Can a Christian Divorce Another Christian For Abuse?* https://rickthomas.net/can-a-christian-divorce-another-christian-for-abuse/

Some people occasionally are manipulative, put others down, and use words that hurt, injure, or wound their spouse. These words and behaviors are characteristics of sinners, as the Bible says humans are (Rom. 3:23).

We are unwilling to label every harmful or hurtful interaction in a problematic marriage as "abuse." We know there are grouchy, cantankerous, ungodly men like Nabal (1 Sam. 25:2 – 4, 25), and we know that there are contentious and vexing women who are equally ungodly (Prov. 21:9, 19). Truth be told, we all can be difficult and even downright mean at times. Emotional and verbal abuse can be hard to prove because it is usually done in the home where there are no witnesses (Deut. 19:15). Unfortunately, some people falsely claim abuse to get revenge on their spouse or control the relationship. How can we be sure abuse claims are valid, and the person is not exaggerating what is happening in their marriage? How do we at Reigning Grace distinguish between "abusive" and someone acting like a "jerk?"

Pastor Chris Moles provides an excellent word picture when he says, "Don't look at the stars; look at the constellation!"[27] Allow us to explain: when we look at the evening sky on a cloudless night, we can see millions of stars that blanket the heavens. They are individual stars until we see patterns that we know as the Big Dipper or Sagittarius. Identifying constellations can be similar to identifying patterns of abuse. In other words, as sinners, we all can exhibit sinful behaviors and use sinful speech (stars) from time to time without it being "abusive."

---

[27] Chris Moles, *The Heart of Domestic Abuse* Course, Module One: *The Extent of the Problem,* Lesson One: *Domestic Violence in the Christian Home: What is Domestic Violence?*

The key is that in abuse, the behaviors are a *pattern* that is *intended* to gain or maintain coercive power and control over another person (constellation). The goal is to intimidate, humiliate, isolate, frighten, terrorize, threaten, or coerce one's spouse. When sinful behaviors are *not* intended to gain or maintain power and control over another, they do not rise to the level of being labeled as domestic abuse. Some sinners are simply selfish, rude, short-sighted, insensitive, and challenging to live with. In other words, a "jerk."

It is essential to protect someone from being falsely accused of being abusive. We listen very carefully to both the husband and the wife, employ the wisdom and discernment that comes from God, and use the tools and resources we have amassed to reach what we believe to be an accurate conclusion about the situation. Our goal is to provide counsel that will bring glory to God and benefit both the husband and the wife.

There are a variety of tools available to evaluate what comprises domestic abuse and violence.

Risk Assessment: Abuse Risk Inventory (ARI)

One tool we use is the Abuse Risk Inventory (ARI) (Appendix A). We have learned that valuable insights will be gained from the comments and stories the counselee shares as they complete the survey. While we record the number of "Yes" responses on the ARI, they alone do not determine if "abuse" occurs in the home. The ARI is only one tool used in the evaluation process, along with our counselee's disclosures, history, and the effects living this way is having on him or her.

The ARI is also helpful when interviewing a person accused of abuse. The counselor can take the accused through each of the statements on a blank ARI, not the spouse's completed one, and learn what specifically they are doing and how often they are sinning against their spouse. It enables the counselor to learn if there are patterns of coercive power and control that would be considered abusive. The use of the ARI sets the stage for further counseling by focusing specifically on the actions and behaviors that need repentance. However, it is essential to understand that the accused may lie, minimize their behavior, blame their spouse, justify and rationalize their actions when questioned or confronted about their behaviors. They may use generalizations such as "sometimes," "occasionally," and "maybe." The ARI provides specificity and clarity in concrete statements that urge the accused to examine their own heart and conscience.

Many abusive men tell me (Bill) that if they filled out the ARI, we would see that *they* are the ones being abused. This also gives him another opportunity to share his side of the story. It is likely true that they have both been brimming with resentments and keeping records of wrongs over the years. Having the husband share his side of the story sometimes reduces some of his defensiveness. He will still minimize and rationalize, but he has just substantiated the need for an intervention.

On occasion, I have had them fill out the ARI and note which behaviors they believe they are guilty of in their marriage. They usually mark about ¼ to ½ of what their wives have checked. This admission only reinforces that they don't have a clue about how their wives experience the treatment they receive.

An abusive husband blindly refuses to believe that the efforts to confront him truthfully about his behavior are out of deep concern and love for him by all who attempt to help him.[28]

The Cycle of Abuse

Some domestic abuse counselors still use the cycle of abuse to describe a pattern or repetitive cycle of behavior that progresses through a build-up of tension, a blow-up or crisis phase, remorse or calm phase, and a repeat of the build-up of tension phase. Each of these phases can last for days or even weeks, and this cycle is repeated repeatedly and, without intervention, will escalate.

Experts in the field no longer recommend using this tool because abuse does not necessarily occur in a cycle. The abuser's reactions and behaviors are not always predictable, and abuse does not typically happen in a tidy order or phases. Additionally, the abuse cycle has been used to blame the victim for not taking action to leave when things are calm.

The Power and Control Wheel

The preferred tool for describing the core tactics of abuse is the Power and Control Wheel.[29] We find this tool to help define and identify many of the actions and behaviors of the abuser. It is not exhaustive but helps both the abuser and the victim understand the heart level motivations and some of the typical tactics used to maintain ungodly power and

---

[28] Debi Pryde and Robert. Needham, *A Biblical Perspective of What to do When You Are Abused by Your Husband,* 4.

[29] Domestic Abuse Intervention Programs, 202 East Superior Street Duluth, Minnesota 55802 218-722-2781 www.theduluthmodel.org

control over the victim. Before discussing the Power and Control Wheel in detail, it is crucial to understand what motivates a person to take these actions and use these tactics.

Power and Control Flow from the Heart

The Bible teaches that the heart is the control center of a human being. It is the immaterial part of a person that contains their thoughts, beliefs, desires, will, emotions, soul, mind, and everything else about a person that we know is there but cannot be touched (Prov. 27:19, 4:23, 1 Sam. 16:7; Matt. 15:19).

The victim often does not want to hold their abuser accountable for the abusive behavior. They want to blame something external like their spouse had a bad family background, poverty, mental illness in the family, or was bullied in school. While some behaviors are learned, the Bible teaches that what comes out of a person reveals what is in their heart. A lousy background or tough upbringing does not excuse abusive behavior (Lk. 6:45).

Power and control emanate from a heart that worships self and is at the core of all abuse forms. The Bible teaches that the actions, attitudes, and words of abuse begin within the heart of the person displaying them. In Mark 7, Jesus said,

> *"Do you not understand that whatever goes into the man from outside cannot defile him, because it does not go into his heart, but into his stomach, and is eliminated?" ...And He was saying, "That which proceeds out of the man, that is what defiles the man. or from within, out of the heart of men, proceed the evil thoughts, fornications, thefts, murders, adulteries, deeds of coveting and*

wickedness, as well as deceit, sensuality, envy, slander, pride and foolishness. All these evil things proceed from within and defile the man." vv. 18-23

Neither counselee may understand the critical role the heart plays in domestic oppression and domestic violence. In Jeremiah 17:9, God says, *"The heart is more deceitful than all else and is desperately sick; Who can understand it?"* This should help us understand passages like Mark 7:20 – 23, Luke 6:45, Matthew 15:18 – 19, and Genesis 6:5. These passages (and more) reveal that, contrary to the world's perspective (the heart is good, and its direction is to be followed), the heart is actually the repository of deceitfulness and wickedness. It cannot be trusted to provide sound biblical guidance. Even the heart of a regenerate Christian contends with evil! If this were not so, Christians would not be deceived into thinking and believing that the aspects of abuse outlined in this book are acceptable. If a Christian's heart were no longer wicked and deceptive, we would no longer sin at all.

The abuser's ultimate goal is to get their emotional and physical desires met, and they selfishly use their partner to fulfill those desires. They do not think about bringing honor and glory to God, their spouse's needs, or discipling their children. They are focused on gaining and maintaining **power** and **control** over their victim. Most abusers are afraid their desires will not be fulfilled through a normal, healthy relationship. Fear motivates them to use abuse to ensure that their desires will be met.[30]

---

[30] Justin Holcomb, & Lindsay Holcomb, *Is It My Fault?* 58.

Abuse is the Fruit of a Deceitful Heart

Luke 6:43 – 45 says,

> *For there is no good tree which produces bad fruit, nor, on the other hand, a bad tree which produces good fruit. For each tree is known by its own fruit. For men do not gather figs from thorns, nor do they pick grapes from a briar bush. The good man out of the good treasure of his heart brings forth what is good, and the evil man out of the evil treasure brings forth what is evil; for his mouth speaks from that which fills his heart.*

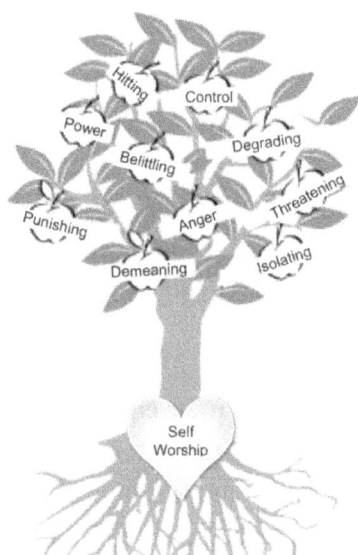

We use a diagram of the tree with both the abuser and the victim to illustrate that abusive behavior (i.e., physical force, intimidation, ridicule, isolation, denial, blame, using the children, male privilege, economics coercion, and threats) is the fruit that flows from the abuser's heart.[31]

When I (Julie) am meeting with a woman I suspect has been abused, as part of the initial meeting with her, I will discuss these verses with her. Sometimes the victim will ask how this (v 43) can be true about her husband. She will point out his good qualities (He's a great dad, a good provider,

---

[31] Chris Moles, *The Heart of Domestic Abuse*, 22-27.

a deacon in the church, etc.) and want to deny he is "abusive" despite the evidence.

A woman who abuses her husband is often hyper-critical. She will rationalize her critical thoughts with statements about his failure to lead, failure to be a godly husband, focus on how he has emotionally withdrawn from her, and then justify berating him (which she calls "helping" or "being honest"). Abusive wives have long and detailed lists of their husband's shortcomings. They become the nagging woman Scripture references (Prov. 27:15-16; 21:19).

The abusive man wants to deny things are as serious as his wife claims they are. He may admit to various behaviors, but he minimizes and adamantly denies he is an abusive husband. Often, he will say he is the victim of his wife. He paints himself as reasonable and the person most invested in the marriage as compared to his wife.

Phil is separated from his wife Jane because he has been emotionally abusive to her for the entirety of their nine years of marriage. He is attending counseling to appease Jane and to get back home.

Phil is very good at pointing out Jane's failure to follow God's plan to reunite with him. He says, "I want the marriage," "I want this marriage back together," "I am going to keep **my** covenant before God" (insinuating Jane is not). He tells the counselor his motives, wants, and desires (to honor God by reuniting with Jane) are godly and biblical.

The counselor realizes Phil self-deceived in his own heart (Jer. 17:9). Phil knows that he has sinned against Jane in the past and vows not to do it again. He has convinced himself that he is doing the godly thing now by standing for the marriage and waiting for her to be ready to reconcile and reunite.

Those are not bad things to want, but the counselor wonders if Phil is standing for the *institution* of marriage rather than standing for what biblical marriage is. The counselor draws Phil's attention to the fruit he has produced and is producing in the marriage. The fruit produced by his wants and desires for his wife and the marriage has proven to be corrupted and rotten. David Powlison says, "The evil in our desires often lies not in what we want but in the fact that we want it too much."[32] Phil wants to preserve the "institution of marriage" and reconcile the marriage rather than doing what it takes to have a biblical marriage.

Phil angrily disagrees with the counselor, but when the fruit of his life is held up to the light of Scripture, bad words and deeds, selfish ambition, evil practices, ungodly thoughts, envy, manipulative plans, and negative attitudes are clearly visible (Jas. 3:14-16). The counselor tries to get Phil to recognize he has dulled his conscience to the significance of what he is doing and the rotten fruit it is producing. The counselor uses Luke 18:9-14, Mark 3:1-6, and Matthew 12:1-5 to confront Phil's pharisaical thinking and conduct in the hope of bringing him to conviction of his ongoing sinful thoughts, beliefs, and actions.

As his sinful heart is revealed, he will repeatedly say to me (Bill) that he doesn't understand why there is a problem. He doesn't see it. He knows she is upset but doesn't know why. She tells him he is abusive, but he disagrees. He admits he has done a few things wrong but denies he is "abusive." He vacillates between telling me he doesn't see the problem (1 Pet. 3:7), and he thinks she is crazy, controlling him, and hyper-critical and that it is his wife who needs counseling, or they need marriage counseling. His desire for marriage counseling is a way for him to control the dialogue and keep the focus on his wife and off his own heart. He wants his wife to be different, and he will deny HE is the problem. I do not attempt to correct his misunderstanding. Instead, I use his concerns to encourage him to continue biblical counseling.

The abusive wife will tell me (Julie) that because her husband doesn't lead the family, she has to do it "because

---

32 David Powlison, *Seeing with New Eyes: Counseling and the Human Condition Through the Lens of Scripture*, P&R Publishing, 149.

someone has to!" She will attempt to manipulate him by berating him, controlling him, buying books on marriage, withholding intimacy, taking him to see the pastor, and demanding he go to counseling.

Both husband and wife must come to see that their actions and words are the fruit of what is going on in their hearts. We help them to identify specific examples of the sin they commit against each other (Matt. 15: 17-20; Gal. 5:19-21). These fruit issues *are* problems, but they are not the *real* problem. The fruit is an indicator of the spiritual matters of the heart. To achieve this awareness and lead to conviction of their sins, we ask the counselee to draw their fruit issues on the tree. We refer to their trees throughout the counseling process. The goal is to help them see that before their actions are sinful, the thoughts, beliefs, and desires of the heart are sinful. These heart issues must be addressed and repented of for any genuine progress to be made.

The tree's illustration shows them their heart must get right with God before anything else in their lives will change. The motive of the heart must change from the worship of self to glorifying God.

Power

Power is a *desire* of the heart. Once a person believes they are entitled to or deserves respect, acknowledgment, to be heard, etc., then they must establish power over another to maintain the illusion of their personal rights. The reality is the heart of a person who abuses is focused on themselves. I (Bill) have found men who abuse and oppress their spouses warp their God-given role as a leader and adopt a selfish, coercive "top-down" approach to leadership that results in control over their wives and children. The fact that these men are often physically bigger makes their tactics for intimidating and controlling their wives (as seen on the Power and Control Wheel) all too effective. These external shows of force reveal self-serving and ungodly heart attitudes.

When the counselee first meets with me and tells me his view of what has happened between him and his wife, he twists the history. To him, it makes perfect sense how she's wrong, and he's right. How he is the victim, and everyone is wrong but him. He doesn't see the problem as his fault-finding, being critical, keeping records of wrongs, and he attempts to make an alliance with me. He struggles to accept 100% responsibility for his part of the problem.

I deal with this by asking the wife to create and send her husband a one- page letter that explains, "This is why I am separated from you." With that letter in hand, in the session, I ask him to respond to what his wife wrote. I note his responses to her letter, which are typically defensive, blaming, and emphasizing her wrongs.

To deal with his denials and justifications, I will compare his responses to David's response to Nathan when he was confronted with his sin.

Have mercy on me, O God, according to your steadfast love: according to your abundant mercy blot out my transgressions. Wash me thoroughly from my iniquity and cleanse me from my sin! For I know my transgressions, and my sin is ever before me. Psalm 51: 1-3. (ESV)

David could have responded to Nathan by claiming his authority as King or blaming Bathsheba for his sin. David did neither of these things but instead took 100% responsibility for his sin before God. He did not retaliate against Nathan, exhibited no defensiveness, and did not blame anyone else for his actions (2 Sam. 11-12:15). This is the pattern we hope the counselee will follow. He will show himself to be a man after God's own heart.

This response differs from he-said-she-said, blaming, and denial, to the fundamental truth that he is totally responsible for his actions and what he has created over the course of their life (Matt. 7: 3-5).

Control

Control is also a *desire* of the heart. Because abusive men believe their wives are needed for their security and significance, they will be highly motivated to act in ways that maintain control over their spouse's thinking and actions. Abusive men will sometimes use overt physical violence, and both abusive men and women use covert "psychological" and verbal intimidation (as seen on the Power and Control Wheel). Sometimes they will use all three as a means to control their victim. The abuser is a master controller, and again, the heart is focused on themselves. Their thoughts, beliefs, and desires are focused on ways to keep their victim "in-line."

I (Julie) have found that women can use many of the same tactics to oppress and control their husbands. Their hearts focus on "being right" and often accuse their husbands of being abusive or failing to lead. Such women attempt to usurp their husbands' God-given authority (Gen. 3:16) by employing various forms of manipulation, emotional abuse, coercion, and using the children (as seen on the Power and Control Wheel).

Anger

Anger is the most common way the abuser *enforces* their power and control. God gave us the emotion of anger that, at times, can be put to a healthy and godly use (Eph. 4:26). However, for violent and abusive people, the release of anger is often used as a tool to further manipulate and exert power over their spouses for their own purposes.

Abusive people typically use various forms of anger and manipulation to maintain power and control, as seen in the Power and Control Wheel's different behaviors. Although not every abusive person will demonstrate all the actions, most will exhibit a pattern (constellation) of several, if not most, of them.

Tactics Used to Gain and Maintain Power and Control

Power and Control Wheel

The Power and Control Wheel is a tool used by secular, Christian and more recently biblical counselors in domestic abuse counseling. Developed in 1984 by the staff at the Domestic Abuse Intervention Project, the Wheel is used in secular counseling to help women identify the actions used against them as abuse. The Wheel is gender-specific and is intended to describe the tactics men use to batter women.

However, we find that because many behaviors are used by both women and men who abuse their spouses, we use this tool differently. It is not brought into the discussion until after we have gathered data from the counselee who self-reports experiencing the tactics described on the wheel. The Wheel is then used to help the victim (whether the man or the woman) understand what they have been experiencing and to realize they are not alone (2 Cor. 1:4; 1 Cor. 10:13). We recognize that the Wheel is descriptive of external actions and motives, but it does not give proper attention to the heart attitudes that prompt those behaviors.

While both men and women can be the perpetrator of abuse, for purposes of clarity and unless otherwise noted, in describing the tactics of abuse below, we will mostly refer to the male as the abuser and the female as the victim.

Abuse can begin with physical and or sexual violence (seen on the outer rim of the wheel), which establishes immediate dominance over the person. Sometimes only one act of physical or sexual violence is necessary to establish dominance and instill fear that it can or might happen again. Other times, the tactics (in the pie pieces) are used to establish and maintain control and power without any physical or sexual violence. One thing is sure, the tactics used by domestic abusers are painful and harmful to the victim and will progress and change as the victim adapts.

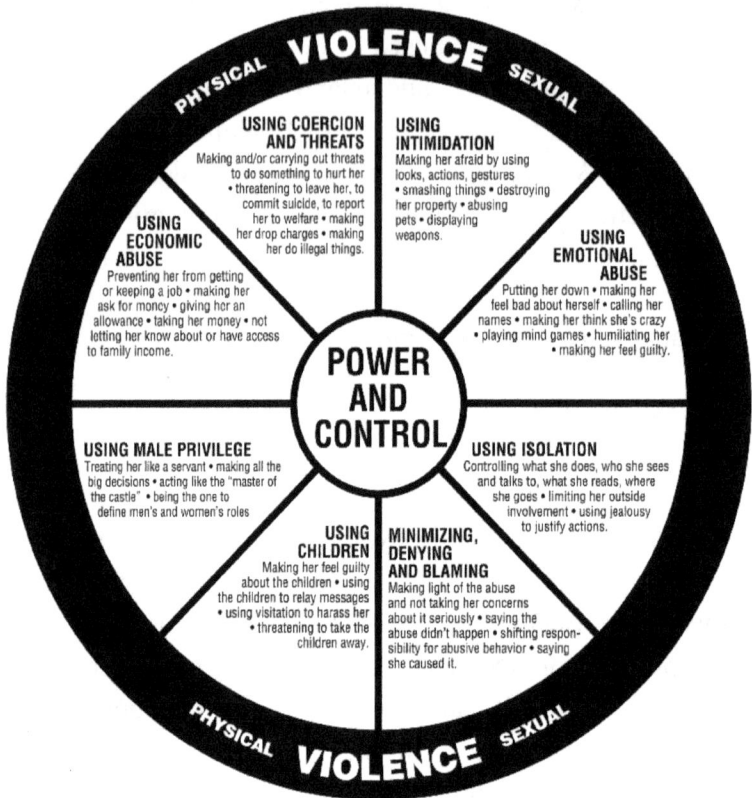

The image is a circular diagram. The outer ring reads: **PHYSICAL VIOLENCE SEXUAL** (top) and **PHYSICAL VIOLENCE SEXUAL** (bottom). The center reads **POWER AND CONTROL**. The wheel is divided into eight segments:

USING COERCION AND THREATS
Making and/or carrying out threats to do something to hurt her • threatening to leave her, to commit suicide, to report her to welfare • making her drop charges • making her do illegal things.

USING INTIMIDATION
Making her afraid by using looks, actions, gestures • smashing things • destroying her property • abusing pets • displaying weapons.

USING EMOTIONAL ABUSE
Putting her down • making her feel bad about herself • calling her names • making her think she's crazy • playing mind games • humiliating her • making her feel guilty.

USING ECONOMIC ABUSE
Preventing her from getting or keeping a job • making her ask for money • giving her an allowance • taking her money • not letting her know about or have access to family income.

USING MALE PRIVILEGE
Treating her like a servant • making all the big decisions • acting like the "master of the castle" • being the one to define men's and women's roles

USING ISOLATION
Controlling what she does, who she sees and talks to, what she reads, where she goes • limiting her outside involvement • using jealousy to justify actions.

USING CHILDREN
Making her feel guilty about the children • using the children to relay messages • using visitation to harass her • threatening to take the children away.

MINIMIZING, DENYING AND BLAMING
Making light of the abuse and not taking her concerns about it seriously • saying the abuse didn't happen • shifting responsibility for abusive behavior • saying she caused it.

When presented as part of the history, physical violence needs to be explored in its entirety with the abuser. Physical violence may include punching (sometimes on the body where it will not show), pinching, shoving, slapping, and the like (Ps. 72:4). Because men against weaker women most often use physical violence, the counselor should inquire about the number of times he used violence against her and the places on her body that he hit her. Did he use an open hand or closed fist? Did he use handheld instruments, did he kick her, etc.? What was the duration of the attacks? Were his wife or children cowering, crying, begging, pleading, hiding, fainting, running away? All of these transgressions need to be documented and acknowledged (Ps. 38:18, Num.

5:7). *"I acknowledged my sin to You, and my iniquity, I did not hide."* Psalm 32:5. It is not unusual for men who use violence against their wives to have developed the habit of blaming others, making excuses, and speaking into their hearts several rationalizations and justifications for their behaviors.

I want to hear more of his thoughts about some of the problems in the marriage. Frequently, these conversations will substantiate the need for biblical counseling and intervention. Some of the commonly used tactics are outlined below.

Playing Mind Games

The wife might describe what we would call mind games. Her initial disclosure will include being told she is "crazy" because she does not recall conversations and arguments the way he does. Her husband might say to her she just imagines something that she is sure was said. He also might insist that she is thinking thoughts she is not and read into what his wife says, twisting her words to mean something different than what she said. She might say her husband gives her mixed messages and tells her she does not make sense. Also, because he keeps telling her that she is crazy and at fault for their marriage problems, she no longer knows what to believe. Her husband makes comments that cause her to be confused and question her sanity. He may even be "gaslighting" her by corroding the foundation of logic upon which she thinks.[33]

John told Josie that people at church, in his family, and some of their friends are

---

[33] Anne Dryburgh, *Debilitated and Diminished: Help for Christian Women in Emotionally Abusive Marriages.* Self Published, 2018, 25.

concerned about her. He said they are talking amongst themselves and are questioning her judgment, questioning her sanity, and asking him what is wrong with her. John suggested she needs help. Josie said she's recently discovered he's been lying to her family and friends about her (creating isolation and divisiveness). One friend helped her see John is making up stories about her and blaming her for his actions.

Gaslighting is accomplished by charm, lies, and manipulation to cause someone to believe in an alternate reality (Prov. 31:30). This causes her to doubt her own perception of things because he so frequently undermines her thinking and conclusions.[34]

We have had husbands refer their wives for counseling regarding these matters. His goal is to perpetuate the charade and get her "fixed" to meet his expectations and standards. He believes the counselor will concur with his assessment of the situation and his wife's deficiencies and tell her she needs to change. "Abusers go to great lengths to portray themselves as morally superior and intellectually more reasonable than their victims. By the time they get to counseling, many victims are so overwhelmed and insecure about themselves that they do, in fact, seem unstable."[35]

Using Male Privilege

Husbands who come in for abuse counseling will frequently accuse their wives of disrespecting them of being unsubmissive (Eph. 5:22-24, 33). Abusers will take the biblical mandate to submit out of context and sinfully use their God-given authority as the leader in the home for

---

[34] DC Robertsson, Blog, *Biblical Perspectives On Narcissism: Recognizing and Dealing With The Evil of Insolent Pride,* 12-6-2017, https://biblicalperspectivesonnarcissism.com/category/3-consequences/3-consequences-for-others/ accessed 6-17-2020

[35] Joy Forrest, *Called to Peace,* 78.

personal gain and to exert power and control over their wives. Pastor Warren Lamb says,

> There is a disturbing correlation between the hyper-headship/patriarchy view of male "headship," male leadership in the home, and domestic oppression, domestic abuse, and sexual abuse.[36]

Their authority in the home is frequently anchored in biblical misinterpretation and is expected to be unquestioned. They consider their wives' questions to be disrespectful and evidence of their rebellion to a husband's authority and leadership. Her suggestion that what he is saying or doing is a misuse of Scripture is met with accusations that her Bible knowledge is inferior to his own, while, in reality, he is twisting the Scriptures to enforce his selfish   agenda.

Bob acts like he is the "Master of the Castle." While Bob has always been somewhat controlling, he recently proclaimed he is the CEO of his family and must oversee every aspect of the home. Bob has always managed the finances for their home, but lately, he has cut off his wife, Mary, from having access to their banking information. He has also started requiring her to produce a log of her daily activities to verify she is spending her time wisely while he is at work.

Recently, he started having Mary and the children line up on Sunday morning before Church to check everyone's clothing choices before they leave home, even though there has not been a problem with modesty. Bob told her she can no longer be friends with women he considers to be bad influences, even though some are women from church and others are neighbors she has been evangelizing.

---

[36] Warren Lamb, *Behind the Veil*, 83.

A husband who asserts male privilege may require his wife to participate in sinful activities, degrading sexual behaviors, force her to lie for him, and, most importantly, keep things secret that are taking place inside the home. The wife might say her husband has special rules for himself that are different from everyone else's and special privileges to which no one else is entitled. To question him shows a lack of respect for his authority and further demonstrates that she is unsubmissive.

Using Isolation

The wife may reveal controlling behaviors such as isolation from her from family and friends.

> The degree to which the husband has managed to isolate his wife, (not only from others but from truth itself), tends to increase her internal struggles as she experiences abuse and as she seeks to make sense out of what has happened or is happening on a daily basis. She may have great difficulty discerning the reality of her husband's manipulation and abuse because she has no one else with whom she can test her perceptions.[37]

The husband may not want his wife to spend time with her parents or siblings without him, but he refuses to go with her to family events. He may tell her she can go alone, but she has learned by experience that when she does this, he makes life miserable for her while she is away. He may repeatedly text message her demanding to know when she

---

[37] Debi Pryde, & Robert Needham, *A Biblical Perspective of What to do When You Are Abused by Your Husband,* 25.

will come home or inventing reasons for her to go home much earlier than the time to which he previously agreed.

When asking about isolation tactics, he may tell me (Bill), "I've never kept her from visiting her family; in fact, she visits them too much." When asked about his behavior, he will redirect the conversation back toward what his wife does or does not do. His statements will typically begin with "She." This is how he relates to his wife—redirecting to focus on what she does or does not do, taking the focus off his own behavior.

Shanise's Grandma phones one evening after Deshawn arrives home from work. Deshawn quickly became angry as soon as he heard Shanise greet her Grandma. He huffed and grumbled about the interruption in his evening to attempt to get Shanise to hang up the call. Shanise pleaded with her eyes to have a few minutes with her grandma. Deshawn pouted, attempted to interrupt the call, and ultimately left the house, slamming the door on his way out. Shanise heard him squeal the tires as he sped off in what she concluded was an angry fit.

Within minutes, Shanise's phone began to blow up with text messages from Deshawn accusing her of not caring about him, not wanting to spend time with him, not respecting him, and accusing her of loving her friends or family more than she loves him.

Men do not exclusively use this tactic; abusive women also isolate their victims. Often an emotionally abused person will confide to the counselor that their spouse does not want their attention to be on anyone but them while they are home. The abusive spouse may use the silent treatment, act hurt or wounded, yell at their husband or wife, accuse their spouse of not loving them, or of being insensitive to their needs. Either spouse may attempt to manipulate with guilt while blaming the other for their loneliness or for feeling unloved.

Using Emotional Manipulation

In addition to what has already been said, abusive men will exert control by showing contempt and making disparaging remarks to their wives. Name-calling, ridiculing, making humiliating statements, using "put-downs" are all tools to exert control. These troubling and debilitating remarks can be relentless and leave the victim doubting their capabilities and even their sanity. *"The fear of the Lord is to hate evil; Pride and arrogance and the evil way and the perverted mouth, I hate."* Proverbs 8:13

Emotional manipulation can and does take on other forms. The husband may disappear for hours or days without informing his wife to frighten her or punish her for some perceived wrong she has done. He may threaten to shoot or cause harm to the family pet. Some men and women use suicide threats as a means of keeping their spouse as their emotional and physical hostage.

Other emotional manipulation methods include sulking and forcing the spouse to play the "what's wrong?" guessing game. These tactics keep the victim on alert and necessitate regularly taking their spouse's emotional temperature and adjusting to "keep the peace." Abused women have told us they could tell if it would be a good or bad day within ten minutes of waking up, depending on their husbands' mood.

GiGi and Tim would have volatile arguments in which he would say, "You don't really love me. I am such a failure as a husband; maybe you would be happier if I just went and killed myself." GiGi would quickly reassure him that she loved him and tell him he is a wonderful husband. Sometimes Tim would threaten to kill himself and then leave home. He would refuse to answer her calls or to return her frantic text messages. He would be gone for hours without a word, leaving GiGi home terrified that he might have killed himself only to eventually return home after he thought he taught her a lesson.

Abusive women manipulate by using massive amounts of words to control their husbands. She taunts him, criticizes him relentlessly, badgers, demeans, and berates him. Some women keep extensive logs and records of his (alleged) offenses against them. They bait their husbands, mind read, assign meanings to his fictitious words, read meaning into what he says, and accuse them of wrongdoing.

Using Sexual Manipulation

Emotionally abused women may confide that their partner typically wakes them up or keeps them up until the wee hours of the morning, having endless, circular discussions about the inadequacy of the love, attention, desire, and care she has for him. It is an endless badgering diatribe of her deficiencies and her failure to love him as he "needs," wants or desires to be loved by her. This is a no-win situation for a wife. Such a man is an emotional bottomless pit, and there is nothing she can say to convince him of her love for him. Every attempt to assure him of her love is met with examples of her failure.

Although his wife is physically and emotionally exhausted from these discussions, it is very common for him to want to conclude these talks with sex so she "can prove to him that she loves him as she says she does." He gives no thought as to whether she is on her monthly cycle, how many hours she has been awake, how soon she will have to wake up, or thought to the lateness of the hour. He also does not take into account the effect his badgering has had upon her emotionally. His expectation is she will joyfully and lovingly comply with his desire for sex. If she does not give him the response he desires, it's another failure, and he repeats the cycle.

Ally confided that Terrell was complaining about her lack of interest in him physically and sexually. She said Terrell tends to be very sexually demanding. She struggles to be sexually stimulated by him because his demands are selfish, and he gives no thought or consideration to her. Sometimes he will want sexual intercourse or sexual play several times a day, regardless of other things going on in the home with the children or with her physical condition. Ally said if she does not immediately and cheerfully comply with Terrell's demand for sex, he will shame, manipulate, blame, and accuse her of not loving him. He said he wants her to initiate sex, but when she does, he complains she is not "doing it right" because she's not aggressive enough. She doesn't say that she "wants him enough."

Some husbands compare their wives to other women or objectify them by ogling, groping, or fondling them at inappropriate times and places. This is body-focused, not person-focused. It is selfish and demeaning, and many women report they "feel like a piece of meat." If he views pornography, she may sheepishly tell me her husband makes demands for unnatural and unbiblical sex acts such as anal intercourse and the introduction of porn into the marriage bed.

Some husbands also use Scripture to manipulate their wives sexually. Using verses like 1 Corinthians 7:4 and 6:19, he coerces his wife into providing sex. When he does this, he is thinking of himself and not his wife. Sex is an arrogant expectation and not the picture of intimacy as the spiritual one-flesh relationship God intends (Eph. 5:31)! There is no mutuality; it is selfish and unloving. She is an object, and he is using her body for his selfish desires. The sexual demands come after a day of the husband being unloving and cruel to his wife. He has shown her no tenderness or love throughout the day, and often he has paid her no attention other than to criticize her.

Using Finances

Economic abuse is another form of emotional abuse frequently used to exert power and to control their spouse. This form of harassment may include withholding money needed for medical care and household management, as well as stealing or sabotaging the victims' job.

Jasmine was ill, and James would not allow her to see a doctor insisting they didn't have the money for their $50.00 insurance copay. She later found receipts from his purchase of a new video game along with the leftovers of a fast-food purchase. When she asked him about these items' cost, James became enraged and told her she was not to question him about money. He stated he is the head of the home and because he works hard for the money, he is entitled to spend it as he sees fit.

The abuser may restrict spending so severely the victim cannot adequately provide for the household. When I (Bill) am taking the abusive husband through the tactics of abuse from the Power and Control Wheel, he usually does two things: He minimizes and outright lies.

For example, when discussing economic abuse, the husband might say, "She has full reign over the checkbook. In fact, she spends money willy-nilly!"

Tiara told her counselor that her husband, Tanner, is completely unreasonable when it comes to the finances. Tiara works full time and is expected to turn over her entire paycheck to Tanner. That's not so bad, but Tanner is so controlling of the money that Tiara says she can't buy the necessary groceries or general merchandise needed to keep the home running. She says Tanner requires a receipt for every item she purchases, including gasoline, or when she takes the children for an ice cream cone. Tanner will also berate her for "wasting" money, being a "poor shopper," and not respecting him because she is a poor steward of the money he provides. Tiara says it is just not possible to provide what is needed on the amount of money he allows her to spend, but he will not accept any of her reasonable pleas for additional funding.

Intimidation

The abuser may also admit that he or she should not get angry or scream or slam doors and request from the counselor socially acceptable ways to get their needs (sinful desires of power and control) met. They appear to be humble and asking for "advice" or "seeking wisdom." In reality, this is a cunning tactic used by those who abuse to attempt to manipulate the counselor, friend, or church leaders to achieve their sinful goals.

Intimidation carries fewer legal consequences than physical violence. It is, however, a very effective and powerful tool in the hands of an abusive person. The victim feels afraid because their spouse uses looks, gestures, stance, volume, and tone of voice to frighten and control them.

Ashley is clearly afraid the day you meet with her. She tells you her appointment must finish on time because she has to be home before Pete gets there. Ashley describes Pete as "crazy." She says she has been living a nightmare since they married three months ago. Ashley doesn't know what to do because Pete has threatened to hurt her if she ever tries to leave or if he ever learns she has told anyone anything about their marriage. She describes living in a virtual prison and constantly on alert, gauging Pete's moods and reactions to every situation because she never knows when or why he will explode. Ashley watches Pete's face and listens for "that tone" he gets right before things "get bad." She denies ever being hit by Pete, but once, he blocked the doorway and took her keys so she couldn't leave during an argument. Pete had already kicked the cat in a fit of rage and broke an antique lamp her father gave her as a gift.

Intimidation establishes power and control over the victim because those experiencing this kind of mistreatment are eventually convinced of their inadequacy. These husbands demean their wives (Prov. 12:18; 16:27) and imply that they are failures as people.

Using the Children

The abusive spouse may also threaten to hurt the children to remind their spouse of their power and control.

> This may include threats to take the children away, using the children to relay messages to the victim, using the children as a means of guilt-tripping, and using visitation rights and custody concerns to harass.[38]

Cletus' wife, Fiona, is verbally and emotionally abusive. When he says he's had enough of how she hurts him and he threatens to leave her, she threatens to accuse him of child sexual abuse. Cletus is terrified she will carry out the threat and says

---

[38] Chris Moles, *The Heart of Domestic Abuse*, 25.

he   stays   to   protect   the   children   from   her.

Using the children is a very common and effective means of keeping an abused spouse in the marriage. A parent will remain in almost any situation to protect their children from harm, even at their own peril. Children become the pawns and are used to achieve the selfish ends of the abusive spouse.

Isabella has filed for legal separation from her abusive husband, Jonas. Her church agrees with Isabella that Jonas has been abusive to her and the children and is unrepentant. Jonas uses their 12-year-old to pass messages to Isabella of his various demands. If she doesn't comply with his demands, he threatens to paint her as unstable, unreasonable, a neglectful mother, and file for the children's full custody.

Because the court system does not always understand abuse dynamics, victims will often continue to be harmed by their abuser even after legal matters are settled. Unfortunately, judges are often persuaded or fooled by abusers who can appear so reasonable and winsome in court. Court-ordered visitation can be a nightmare for the abuse victim as he or she must regularly engage with their abuser when exchanging the kids or interacting with them. Parenting plans often leave room for the parents to interact with each other regarding their children. This provides the abusive spouse or ex-spouse an avenue to continue to frighten, intimidate, and inflict pain on the victim.

Responding to Physical Violence: Helping the Victim

While it is usually the woman who is physically assaulted in an abusive marriage, wives can and do physically abuse their husbands. The initial steps for helping a person impacted by domestic violence are very practical.

Medical Care

Domestic violence affects women in a variety of ways. Five key feelings commonly experienced by emotionally abused women are fear, shame, guilt, anger, and feeling like they are "going crazy."[38] Men who have been abused feel ashamed, fear, worry, lonely, inadequate, demeaned, numb, isolated, insecure, and struggle with trust. These emotions affect a victim's health and physical body.

The initial steps for helping a person impacted by domestic violence are very practical. We must make sure that she and any children are safe from harm and in a living situation that will be stable enough for her to participate in the biblical counseling process (Prov. 22:3, 24:11; Ps. 82:4). Therefore, physical separation, sometimes long-term, often becomes necessary.

To mandate that a woman remains in the home with her abusive husband allows him to continue to sin against her, perpetuating the abuse. His presence in the home enables his sinful heart attitudes to continue to be acted out on his wife.

> If a separation is needed for safety, then strongly reinforce to the abused spouse that she should expect intense pressure to return home (anger, shaming, promises, and so on). The question 'How can we work on the marriage if they are not in the same home?' is a

manipulative one. It dodges the fact that the primary problem is abuse.[39]

Those who have experienced domestic violence are likely to experience a wide range of health problems. For this reason, it is always wise to recommend they get a medical exam and begin treatment for any physical complications brought on by physical or emotional abuse.

There may be resistance to involving medical personnel because of what may be revealed through an examination. Abused women are fearful and suspicious and many have been conditioned to be that way by their spouse. There may be concern over being diagnosed with a "mental illness" that could affect her ability to maintain custody of the children.

Physical Safety

Because physical domestic violence can be a life-or-death matter, the counselor must do everything in their power to ensure the safety of a woman and any children. While she is in the office, we must learn when her husband last assaulted or battered her.

When physical abuse has occurred, it is wise to encourage her to document present and future events with pictures, recordings, dates, and times he has exhibited abusive behaviors. A good rule to remember is, "if it is not documented, it does not exist." Take pictures of any injuries, weapons, or property destruction, including the room where the violence occurred. This includes punching things (holes in the walls, pillow, etc.) without hitting her, breaking things, and threatening physical harm to her or himself. This creates

---

[39] Brad Hambrick, *Self-Centered Spouse: Help for Chronically Broken Marriages.* (Phillipsburg: P & R Publishing Company, 2014), 22.

a paper trail and a record of escalation and pattern of abusive behavior. It will be helpful should her husband minimize or deny his mistreatment of her. She should not keep this documentation on her phone or computer but forward it to a safekeeping person. She should then delete it from her devices and empty the "trash," so he cannot find it if he searches her phone or emails.

Abused wives typically know their abusers' patterns and often can (but not always) predict when they will be volatile. If her husband is not presently acting out in violence, she may think it is safe to remain in the home. While you cannot recommend she return or live in a home where physical abuse has taken place, you can trust her judgment to be there just long enough to put pieces in place to make it easier for her to flee when it is time.

Pryde and Needham say,

> Many abused wives have realized, in retrospect, that in each of these cycles of abuse, there was a gradual buildup of tension before the next explosion occurred. They couldn't always put their finger on it, but they often sensed when a violent outburst was coming and felt powerless to do anything about it.[40]

Domestic Violence is a Crime

When a husband uses physical force against his wife, that is a crime and should be reported to the police. Some counselors and pastors are mandated reporters, so it is wise

---

[40] Debi Pryde, & Robert Needham *A Biblical Perspective of What to do When You Are Abused by Your Husband,* 24.

to determine ahead of time if this is the law in your area. We can only urge reporting; we cannot force her to do it unless children or the elderly are being abused. When children or the elderly are being abused, the law mandates this gets reported to the authorities (Rom. 13:1-7).

Before going to the police station, help her understand the importance of filing a police report and pressing charges. She may express fear at exposing him and even become angry at you for suggesting this measure of safety. We recommend you offer to accompany your counselee to the police station and stay with her as long as the authorities will allow.

We cannot overemphasize the importance of pressing charges! If she does not take this step, he will be released from jail and quickly return home. She will be in tremendous danger from him. Pressing charges forces him to be held accountable for his actions (Rom. 13:1-7). The victim may ultimately refuse to have him arrested or press charges, even when physical violence is taking place in the relationship. It is *vital* to communicate to her that reporting him and holding him accountable is the first step in *helping* her husband (Gal. 6:1-2; Heb. 10:24). Being arrested will show him that his actions are serious, but it will do nothing by itself to change him. This is not vengeance or sinful, but, instead, it is a loving act intended to bring her husband to repentance and address his sinful behavior (Gal. 6:1; Jas. 5:19-20).

Create a Safety Plan

When there is potential for violence, or if the counselee believes she may have to flee, I (Julie) help her to create a safety plan while in the office (Appendix B). Many items on the safety plan do not need to be completed for short-term separation or in cases where violence has not occurred. The wife should be aware of all of these recommendations and have a general idea of how, if necessary, to quickly complete a safety plan. The counseling team should advise the victim on the appropriate course of action based on her situation (Ps. 82:1-8; Prov. 11:14; 15:22; 24:6).

The safety plan contains specific tasks for the wife to accomplish before leaving her home. These tasks need to be completed while her husband is away, and she is confident he will not come home and catch her preparing to flee. If there is ongoing physical abuse taking place in the home, I do not recommend that she return to the house alone. If an escort is needed, I have her use my office phone to call the police non-emergency number to get a police escort. The police will stay with her as she packs up the items she will need after leaving home.

Secure Weapons

To ensure all parties' safety, determine if the abuser has any firearms or other weapons that could be used for deadly force and secure those weapons outside of the home, if possible.

Prepare to Flee: Pack a "Go-Bag."

One of the safety plan tasks is to pack a "go-bag" with enough clothes, medications, and personal items for herself and her children to last several days. She should put it in a safe place that she is confident her abuser will not discover. Some suggestions would be leaving it at the home of a trusted neighbor, the church office, the pastor's home, a friend's home, or another place away from her house but easily accessible to her if she must flee in a hurry.

The complete list of items she should have in the go-bag is in the safety plan. The sooner the woman can begin to gather these items, the better. Some of the more critical things to get together are essential documents that she will need to provide identification or get assistance.

For some documents, such as Social Security cards, passports, birth certificates, driver's license, and immigration papers, only originals will do. She should have a clear idea of where these documents are kept so she can grab them quickly. Other documents such as vehicle information, mortgage papers, medication, immunization records, and other things on the list can be photocopied ahead of time and kept in the go-bag in a Ziploc baggie to protect them from accidental water damage.

Financial Needs

If physical violence requires a separation, the woman will need funds to live and care for herself and any children. It is not always possible for a wife to access funds held in a banking institution (the abusive husband designs it that way). She will need **cash** and not credit cards when she flees. Credit cards provide a paper trail of her actions and location. It is unwise to use them when escaping an abusive partner. Be cautious when converting cash to prepaid cash cards (Visa, MasterCard) because some of these cards carry hefty transaction or user fees when you use them, and some of them even expire!

It is wise to open a bank account for her safety and financial security in her own name. She must alert the bank not to send any correspondence to her home! If she can't open her own account, or if she does not have access to the family bank account, the wife should attempt to set money aside that her husband will not miss. The money should be kept in the go-bag. If her husband keeps all the cash on lockdown, she may have to depend on her church or friends to give her money until she can get to safety and get on her feet financially. The church should create an emergency fund specifically for this purpose (Isa. 25:4; 1 Jn. 3:17-18).

Secure Transportation

Some husbands do not put their wives' names on any property, including a car. Putting everything in only his name allows him maximum control over her and limits her ability to escape the situation. As a part of her plan to flee, the church may need to provide her with a vehicle to access in a hurry. Be advised, taking the family car allows him to trace her by reporting it stolen, especially if her name is not on the title.

Change Phones

As she prepares to flee, I advise caution when making phone calls on a cell phone. She will want to leave no hint or trace of her activity, and many people forget that every phone call is listed on the monthly cell phone bill. If she is making calls to domestic violence shelters or doing other preparatory work, it is wise to borrow a phone or use a public landline.

When it is time to run, it is vital that she turn off the locator on her cell phone and other electronic devices she carries on her person. Many women do not realize they are being tracked everywhere they go because their phone's location setting is on. If turning off the location device would arouse suspicion, she should leave the locator turned on and leave the phone at home when she flees.

I recommend obtaining a "burner phone" from a big box store to contact those she needs to speak with and personal safety. Very few people should have this phone number. I suggest using the*67 feature to block caller ID when making a phone call to anyone except the one or two people who will know her whereabouts. If the phone has internet capability, be sure that no location devices are enabled for text messaging, phone calls, or email.

Find Shelter

When there is physical violence in the home, the woman may need to find a place to hide from her abusive husband. Well-meaning family and friends can offer her and her children a place to stay, but this is not always a wise decision as he may stop at nothing to find her and bring her home. If her place of shelter is known to her abuser, it is almost certain that he will look for her there, and it may put not only her but the individual sheltering her in a great deal of physical harm. When an abuser is denied access to his victim, he may become more dangerous. Approximately 75% of domestic homicides occur while the victim is trying to leave their abuser or has just left the relationship.[41]

For this reason, whenever possible, a woman should go to a place of safety outside of her immediate area. If the

---

[41] Justin Holcomb, & Lindsay Holcomb, *Is It My Fault?* 65.

couple has children in common, I do not recommend leaving the state because the father has a legal right to see his children. Even if she is fleeing for her safety, the woman may be considered a kidnapper if she leaves the state with her children.

She may initially need to go to a shelter for abused women for her safety until she can make arrangements to go elsewhere. Most women are reluctant to go to a shelter. In fact, even women living through ongoing abuse often would rather stay in the home and wait it out than go to a shelter. If there is no other option, she should attempt to get into a shelter even if it is not her preference.

The shelter will provide immediate safety and security for her and her children from the abuser (Prov. 22:3). Many shelters offer access to medical care and free legal counsel. It will be helpful for her to have her go-bag with her, especially since it will contain vital papers to help her navigate the legal system. This is the benefit of putting this together ahead of time and storing it until needed.

Women's shelters are experts at helping women obtain an order of protection and other services that are needed in the early days after she leaves an abusive situation. These shelters also provide counseling for women and children. While the advice offered is secular in nature, it may benefit her and the children to be educated on domestic violence.

Get Legal Help

The wife may need to obtain legal counsel after separating from the violent abuser and arriving at a place of safety (Prov. 11:14; 15:22; 20:18; 24:6). She may need to file for a legal separation, an order of protection, child support, if needed, and any necessary public assistance. She may or may not need legal representation for these actions. It varies from state to state.

We are often asked the reason we suggest filing for a legal separation. To be clear, our goal is *always* reconciliation whenever that is possible. However, it is common for the abuser to attempt to manipulate her to come home and demonstrate his power and control over her by draining bank accounts, threatening her, and harassing her, all to force her to return home.

If there are children involved, we want her to return to the home as quickly as possible because this is often in her best interests and the children's best interests. Without a legal separation, making her the home resident, in some states, the wife has no legal right to keep her abuser off the property and protect herself and the children from any further abuse.

Also, legal separation and protection orders are necessary to prevent the abuser from terrorizing his wife by coming onto the property whenever he feels like it. Legal documents will allow her to change the locks on the doors to prevent his entry at will, may provide child support funds for the children, and might include a temporary custody and visitation schedule for the children. The order may stipulate other actions the husband must take to provide for the welfare of the children.

A woman who does not stay in the home should be aware that she may have the right to request that her new address is not disclosed in court documents. This, too, may vary from state to state. Many states participate in the "Safe at Home" program, in which victims of domestic violence and other crimes can conceal their new address. The program allows domestic abuse victims to establish a post office box (usually in her state's capital city). All her mail will be received there and forwarded to her actual address. Victims of domestic violence should take advantage of the wide range of free services that are offered. These services are also available to those who do not stay in a shelter.

Plan for the Immediate Future

If a long-term separation is necessary, once the immediate needs of safety and shelter have been addressed, the woman will need to find suitable long-term housing, transportation, employment, and possibly childcare. This may be challenging if the woman has no marketable skills to provide enough income to be self-supporting. The church may need to financially support the woman in part or total as she gets her life together. Church members can help by providing a car for her to use, free or low-cost housing, furnishings, and essentials for her new home, and childcare as she enters the workforce.

Separation for Non-Violent Abuse

> *If your right hand makes you stumble, cut it off and throw it from you; for it is better for you to lose one of the parts of your body, than for your whole body to go into hell.*
> Matthew 5:30

Jesus certainly was not suggesting in Matthew 5:30 that a person maims themselves; He was indicating that God takes *all* sin seriously. As previously stated, emotional and verbal abuse is sin, and sometimes drastic measures are needed to help an abusive person understand the gravity of their actions.

We recognize that there are many approaches and opinions on how to counsel couples in which there are habitual, excessive, and destructive patterns of emotional and verbal abuse. Sometimes these coercive controlling words and behaviors have instilled fear, broken the spouse down physically and emotionally, and confused the victim to the point they think they are crazy. In such incidences, we have found a period of physical separation (whether it is short-term or long-term) to be critical to de-escalate the tension in the relationship and for counseling to begin.

The time apart is partially a cooling-off period and provides safety from retaliation or ongoing abuse. Typically, we will ask the husband to stay with a friend or relative for the first few weeks of the counseling process. While the couple is separated, the counseling team will hear from both parties and get a clearer picture of what is taking place in the home (Prov. 18:13, 15, 17). We will begin to address the abused person's confusion and distress while confronting the controlling and manipulative behaviors of the abuser.

Biblical counselors Debi Pryde and Robert Needham were asked, "Isn't separation an overly disruptive means of correcting the problem? Is there a way to deal with the problem without separating?"[42]

> If correcting the problem requires a period of physical separation until the husband has not only admitted his sin, but received real help in overcoming it, is that not a small price to pay for the long-term restoration of the

---

[42] Debi Pryde, & Robert Needham, *A Biblical Perspective of What to do When You Are Abused by Your Husband,* 73.

marriage, protection of the family, and possibly the salvation of his soul? (Proverbs 22:3).[43]

We wholeheartedly agree with this approach. We are interested in the reconciliation and restoration of each couple, but it is essential to recognize that some problems cannot be solved when the couple is together. Our experience has shown us that a period of separation can help facilitate repentance and change. Living apart provides each spouse an opportunity to focus on their relationships with God without the other's interference to fuel their own flames of bitterness and condemnation (1 Cor. 7:5).

We understand that separation is controversial to some pastors, especially when our stated goal is reconciliation. We recognize that this appears counterintuitive. However, we have seen the effectiveness of separation and believe it can be one of the most beneficial counseling process aspects. Pryde and Needham address this critical issue this way:

> Some Bible-believing pastors are so afraid of sanctioning any kind of separation (quoting 1 Corinthians 7:5) that they fear they are disobeying God if they encourage it for any reason whatsoever. They frequently state: "Nowhere in the Bible does God sanction separation." Yet here is a situation where the duty to preserve life and to protect the helpless must take precedence over a wonderfully true principle that applies except when a wife, and sometimes even the children, are in real danger, spiritually, emotionally, and physically (Micah 6:8; Acts 20:35; Romans 15:1; 1 Thessalonians 5:14).[44]

Suppose it is clear that a long-term separation is needed, such as in the case of severe abuse. In that case, we

---

[43] Ibid. 73.
[44] Ibid. 10.

recommend that the couple remain separated through the repentance and part of the reconciliation phase. It takes time for the abusive person first to recognize their sinful heart attitudes and begin repenting of the thoughts, beliefs, and desires that have been a part of their lives for many years. In most cases, these are lifelong issues, and it is unrealistic to expect or anticipate change will occur in a week, a month, or even several months. However, every situation is different. We have a responsibility to the victim to ensure (as much as anyone can) that their spouse will not resume abusive patterns of behavior once reconciliation and reunification are complete.

Consider Restricting Contact

It is wise to consider restricting contact between the couple when it is clear that one or both are engaged in sinful patterns of habitual, excessive, and destructive behaviors (Matt. 5:30). You may also uncover that one spouse has been exerting coercive power and control over the other. Often, the couple's previous attempts at solving their problems and correcting their communication have failed. When these things are present, consider cutting them off (for a time) from their ability to continue that sinful behavior.

To some counselors and pastors, restricting contact may seem to be an extreme response. They are squeamish about restricting contact between a husband and wife, citing 1 Corinthians 7. We agree! We also believe that abuse is extreme. In many cases, both the husband and wife's habits are so deeply ingrained that they genuinely do not know how to respond differently to each other. In most of our counseling cases, the couple has previously received marriage counseling, been instructed in communication, managing anger, bitterness, and forgiveness, and yet there is no positive change. Over time, things have escalated beyond arguing and disagreements; the abuser is hurting their spouse physically, emotionally, and possibly sexually. Things have not gotten *better* with communication and interaction; they have gotten *worse*. Their communication is dishonorable, self-serving, and often cruel. They tear each other down, lie, and discourage each other. They are foolish, gossips, and slanderers. (Eph. 4:29: Pr. 15:2; Pr. 18:21; Pr. 18:2; Pr. 13:3; Col. 3:8). By this point, the victim (usually the wife) is being hurt and is often broken down physically and emotionally to the point they think they are crazy. Things between the couple have become harmful, destructive, and abusive.

In addition, a husband who abuses his wife is a master manipulator and has trained her to respond to his verbal and nonverbal cues. He knows if he cleverly twists her words, she will accept the blame in any confrontation. He has become a master at sulking, the adult temper tantrum, and the silent treatment when she tries to address a concern. He undermines her confidence in thinking biblically, and twists Scripture to support his behavior, and uses other forms of manipulation that must be discontinued for progress to be made. This cycle is almost impossible to break when the couple continues to interact with each other.

Often abuse does not end when the couple separates. Without exception, every abuser we have counseled has attempted to maintain power and control over his wife, even after they have been physically separated, by excessive text messaging, voicemails, and email.

Danielle was advised by her pastor to leave home for her safety. When Don discovered she had left, he began barraging her with hundreds of text messages, dozens of voicemail messages, and emails every day. The texts and voicemail messages were accusing, threatening, demanding, and full of harsh words interspersed with his tearful pleas for her to return home. He alternated promising not to hurt her again in one message and threatening her with what would happen if she didn't return home immediately in a different message.

He threatened to kill himself if she didn't comply with his demands and told her it would be her fault if he died. Danielle was confused and unsure of how to respond. She was afraid to stay away from home; she was scared he would really take his own life. He sounded so desperate and as though he was contrite. She thought maybe this time, things would be different. No sooner did she think about heading home, and Don would send another message accusing her of being at fault for his anger and calling her horrible names. He demanded to know where she was. Although Danielle asked him many times during the day to stop messaging her, he continued to blow up her phone with these calls and messages all day and all night.

These messages are usually criticisms of her, harsh judgments, threats, innuendo, and voicing of suspicions. They are intended to terrorize her, keep her in line, and coerce her into coming home (Ps. 55:3; 73:8). He can still control her, instill fear in her, manipulate her, and focus on *her* instead of focusing on his own sinful heart and his need for repentance and change.

Restricting contact is the fastest and most effective means of breaking the power and control pattern the abuser has over the victim. It completely strips them of their ability to control and manipulate their spouse by phone or in-person, and we have found it to be very beneficial for both parties.

Victims describe being in a "fog" and unable to think clearly or objectively (Ecc. 4:1). They struggle to assess their situation or respond to their spouse competently because the narrative changes with every incoming message. This keeps the victim off balance and confused about how to respond. A complete break from the daily power and control opens their eyes to the patterns of abuse, manipulation, and domination their spouse has had over them. It helps them gain clarity about their situation, what they have been subjected to, and their responses to these things.

Allowing one spouse to continue abusing the other by the method of text message and email does not protect them, nor does it help them to focus on repentance and change in their heart. It is never to be used as a "punishment"; it is a tool that will encourage the couple to focus on the issues of their own heart before God. We have found much of the most significant work done when the abuser cannot focus on their spouse or any sinful responses they may have.

When an abusive husband comes to an appointment, I (Bill) am prepared for him to complain and fault-find. He will blame his wife, and he will blame us for keeping her from him. He will often use the Word of God to confront me for "sinning" by initiating the separation and keeping them apart. I remain firm and point out that his wife is afraid of him even if he has not been physically abusive. His attempts to remedy the problems between them have not worked to date. The abusive spouse's inability to communicate with their victim may infuriate them. They will attempt to bully, threaten, intimidate, and manipulate everyone on the counseling team to re-establish contact. The separation and restricted contact will continue until he repents and changes. His anger is additional evidence of his intent to maintain power and control.

"One of the most common characteristics of an abusive person is a passionate defensiveness that takes on many forms. An abuser will vehemently deny he is abusive and will react to any attempt to confront him honestly with such forceful or skillfully manipulative denial that he successfully prevents disclosure or interference with his behavior, sometimes for a lifetime."[45]

A time of separation and no contact also reveals a lot about the abusing spouse. We often see the violent heart on full display during this time as they are denied what they want most of all, which is power and control over their partner (Jer. 17:9; Mk. 7:21-23; Lk. 6:45). If he is allowed to interact with his wife, he may try again to manipulate her by saying he "got counseling" to get her back home with him. When the interaction between them is permitted, progress will be minimal. We strongly urge those assisting couples with domestic abuse to consider restricting contact between the spouses for a while. This, more than anything else, will expose the level of power and control the abuser has over their victim.

A Word About Text Messages

We recognize that nearly everyone has a cell phone in our culture, that communication by text message is a convenient way to "talk." We have found this to be one of the most destructive, divisive, and complicating forms of interaction between people, especially spouses in troubled marriages. We *strongly* believe that texting should be limited to the benign, such as, "Please pick up bread and

---

[45] Debi Pryde, & Robert Needham, *A Biblical Perspective of What to do When You Are Abused by Your Husband*, 20.

milk on your way home." Unfortunately, texting has become a platform on which serious conversations take place. This, more than almost any other form of communication, brings complications and devastation to the relationship. Texting has become an all too common method for couples to talk with each other about serious marital problems, and there is little that is beneficial about it.

Pat: You don't initiate with the kids.
Jamie: Yes, I do.
Pat: No, you don't.
Jamie: Yes, I do! I wanted to see them last Friday, and you said I could, but then you changed your mind at the last minute.
Pat: Well, I got to thinking maybe it wasn't a good idea for you to see them.
Jamie: But then you can't say I don't initiate with the kids!
Pat: See! There you go blaming me again! You said you've changed, but this proves you haven't.
Jamie: Yes, I have! How can you say that? I am doing everything you asked me to do! I am going to counseling like you wanted me to!
Pat: Oh! So, you are only going because I made you go? You don't really think you need help?
Jamie: I am going because I want our marriage and the kids.
Pat: Oh, so you are only going because you want to get back in the house? See! I knew you haven't changed!

Texting is a "flat" form of interaction and does not allow for gathering important data such as intent, tone, inflection, and body language. It provides a means for making assumptions and questioning the motives behind what is said. Texting utilizes "hit and run" and "gotcha" statements, which allow the sender the freedom to say hurtful and inflammatory things without accountability for how those words will affect the receiver. When used this way, it is a form of corrupt communication (Eph. 4:25, 29, 31; Col. 3:8).

Texting continues a pattern of misleading

communication: it furthers the dialogue that doesn't work. We urge all our counselees to stop texting each other and use the method below instead.

Ensuring Contact with Children

We recognize the importance of both parents being involved in the lives of their children. The effects of separation and restricted contact between the adults should have as limited an impact on the children as possible. To ensure communication between parents and children, we recommend using one of the internet applications designed for that purpose. We recommend the app, OurChildInfo.com.[46]

> OurChildInfo.com is a private, secure website used by parents to communicate directly with each other about their child. Posts, replies, documents, and photos cannot be deleted by either parent. OurChildInfo.com is the answer to lost phones, deleted messages, insulting texts, emails, voicemails, verbal agreements. A central communication resource that is verifiable "Written Notice". Court orders, photos, medical bills, school records, sports schedules and any other information or evidence can be provided. Posts by both parents can be seen by the other parent. Every post is automatically tagged by poster, time and date. The site serves as a record of shared information, or ignored questions.[47]

We have found that this app, and others like it, provide a way for parents of children to be involved in their children's lives while protecting them from ongoing abusive communication. It makes it possible for both parents to be made aware of concerns regarding their children. The couple

---

[46] https://www.ourchildinfo.com/

[47] Ibid. accessed 8-27-2020.

can also communicate about necessary bills and other issues that married people need to discuss. Because what is entered is unalterable, if either party uses abusive or coercive speech, it will be in writing and available as evidence if necessary. We have found that our abusive counselees are less likely to put things in writing if they know their words can be shared with a judge or law enforcement.

Though initially, this can be cumbersome and awkward, once they have adapted to it, they are grateful for the respite from the abusive contact and can begin to think and process. This enables counseling to move forward and not be hindered by the clutter and chaos of their sinful interaction patterns.

Supervised Contact

We have learned the importance of supervised and controlled interaction between the spouses during the period of limited contact. After the counseling process is underway, the counselors should arrange a supervised contact group meeting for the couple to interact with each other in a controlled environment such as Zoom. The purpose of supervised interaction is to minimize the back and forth, "he said she said" situation from developing as each counselee interacts with the counselors. This will also help move the counseling forward and prevent hardness of heart from taking root in the spouse suffering from the abuse.

When the wife is the abused party, she is usually hesitant to meet or talk with her husband. She is fearful. Using a video application like Zoom will give the counselors more control over the participants and the meeting's direction and provide a physically safe and secure setting for the abused spouse. The meeting Host can mute and unmute the participants and turn on and off the video if necessary.

Why Do They Stay?

The reasons people stay in abusive marriages are complex, and there are more than we can list. We have identified some of the frequently stated reasons our counselees give us for staying in the relationship.

Religious Conviction

Religious conviction is a primary reason Christians stay in abusive marriages. It is not wrong to have faith and believe God can change an abusive spouse; God can do anything (Lk. 1:37)! What makes our approach to this terrible problem different is we believe that a person who abuses *can change* if they truly desire to honor and glorify God by how they live their lives. Change generally doesn't happen when sin is kept secret. So abusive behavior must be exposed to the light (Eph. 5:11-14). We understand some abuse recipients fear exposing their husband or wife's treatment out of a misguided belief it would be sinful to do so (Rom. 12:21). However, somebody must expose such ungodly behavior for the benefit of both the victim and the perpetrator of abuse (Eph. 5:11-13; Lk. 5:32).

Denial

A common reason people accept being treated in such an ungodly manner is they don't realize they are in an abusive relationship. They don't want to believe the one they love is abusive. These spouses have become experts at denial. They tell themselves what they experience isn't abuse even when there is a clear, cruel, and harmful treatment pattern.

Adaptation

Another reason people remain in abusive marriages is that they have learned to adapt. They have learned how to manage the home and the children in an attempt to minimize conflict. He or she tries to soothe and pacify their abusive spouse, to keep them happy and content.

Lack of Resources

A lack of resources or financial options is typically a problem for women who married young, had children early in the marriage, and have little earning potential. They see no way to support themselves and their children apart from their husband's income.

Fear

Fear is overwhelming. The victim may fear: doing the wrong thing, reprisals if the abuse is revealed, sinning against God, breaking up the family, further abuse, not being supported by other family members or the church, fear of being alone, just to name a few of the most common fears we have noted.

Involving the Church

Form a Team

It is not wise, nor is it always possible for the counselors themselves to attend to every detail involved in a domestic abuse/violence case. Moses' father-in-law Jethro said to Moses, *"The thing that you are doing is not good. You will surely wear out, both yourself and these people who are with you, for the task is too heavy for you; you cannot do it alone"* Exodus 18:17-18. This is wise counsel for those who work with domestic violence or oppression cases. There are so many details to be worked through, especially in the early stages of counseling, that the counselors can quickly be overwhelmed and distracted from their primary responsibility, providing soul care. Jethro counseled Moses by advising him this way,

> *Now listen to me: I will give you counsel, and God be with you. You be the people's representative before God, and you bring the disputes to God, then teach them the statutes and the laws, and make known to them the way in which they are to walk and the work they are to do. Furthermore, you shall select out of all the people able men who fear God, men of truth, those who hate dishonest gain; and you shall place these over them as leaders of thousands, of hundreds, of fifties and of tens. Let them judge the people at all times; and let it be that every major dispute they will bring to you, but every minor dispute they themselves will judge. So it will be easier for you, and they will bear the burden with you.* Vs. 19-22

Jethro's counsel to his son-in-law is transferable to those working with domestic violence and oppressive counselees. Domestic abuse cases often require involvement beyond providing biblical counseling services.

We desire to work with the church, involve them when following the *Roadmap,* and involve them in the counseling process, especially if the pastor or elders referred the couple to us for counseling (Prov. 11:14; 15:22; 24:6). Forming a team enables us to focus on providing the counseling services and provides a division of labor among those in the couple's church who are skilled in the various areas of need. Each team member plays a vital part in helping the couple on the path toward reconciliation and reunifying the family.

When the church is less involved, the team members can come from wise and discerning godly friends or family members. Neither of these is the best option as alliances often develop, and the team members begin "working" for one side. It is our opinion that it is best to have impartial persons function in these roles whenever possible.

Counselors

The counselors' role should be to work with the husband and wife in the process of biblical change to benefit the couple and their children. We encourage the counselors to act as overseers of the counseling team and work alongside and cooperate with their church elders.

The counselors should contact the pastor/elder during or after the first meeting with the counselee. We want him to know that his people have come to us for help. We want to hear his perspective and what counsel he has already offered the couple. We are, of course, interested in knowing if they have followed through with previous counsel.

This meeting can be critical as it allows the counselors to explain their counseling paradigm and learn the church leadership's understanding of abuse dynamics. Establishing a relationship with the church will help the counselee(s) and will demonstrate to the church that you desire to assist them in shepherding their sheep for this period of time. We stress that the counseling goal is to bring God glory through repentance and change that leads to reconciliation and reunification of the family whenever possible.

We enlist the pastor/elders' help with creating the rest of the team that will surround the couple in need. In the first few meetings, we will discuss our counseling plan for the couple with the pastor and seek his input and endorsement. We also ask the pastor to recommend candidates for the team positions and request he contact them and gain their agreement to be a part of the team.

The counselor's responsibility is to keep the pastor and elders informed of the progress, or lack thereof, of the counselee's biblical change and repentance process. We have worked with some pastors who ask us for occasional updates, and others want weekly or monthly updates. The counselors will meet regularly with the Mediator and the counselee's Mentors to discuss issues, progress, failures, and situations that arise with the counselees.

Pastor/Elder

We believe that every pastor who has taken on pastoral care knows the burden of caring for those in difficult and often tragic situations such as those found in domestic abuse and violence. In our experience, we have found that while they desire to help, they often don't fully understand the dynamics of abuse, whom to believe, or how to best help the couple and their children (1 Pet. 5:1-3).

We agree with the suggestion's biblical counselor Sherry Alchin has put together. We will discuss the practical application of these suggestions elsewhere. Alchin says the church should assure the victim that the church will do all it can to protect and support them.[48] This includes providing a safe house for the victim and children if necessary.[49] The church should provide spiritual support by helping the victim

---

[48] Sherry Alchin, *Helping Women Who Have Experienced Domestic Abuse*, Light in the Darkness, ACBC Annual Conference, 2018.
[49] Ibid.

make decisions, involving them in Bible study and accountability, and praying with and for them.[50] Finances can be very problematic when the victim is a woman who has been driven from her home or when there is not enough income to support two households in case of separation. The Pastor can encourage the church to provide funds for rent, food, or children's needs. He can also help find volunteers to help her if she is living in a home that needs repairs (Matt. 25:35-40).[51]

Another critical component of the pastor/elder's role in the counseling process is their willingness to implement biblical church discipline should there be no repentance for sin (Matt. 18:15-17).

Mediator

When separation is deemed necessary, we suggest finding a willing person with sound financial and verbal skills, mature, level-headed, and wise to function as the mediator between the husband and wife. Details on the mediator's role and function are found in *Beginning Framework– Mediator Guidelines* (Appendix C), and *Communication Guidelines* (Appendix D). As you can imagine, the relational dynamics between the couple are difficult and even hostile. Suppose one or both counselees have a history of violence. In that case, the only option available for mediation and addressing the day-to-day problems, issues with children, and finances may be through the court system (Rom. 13). Otherwise, a mediator from the church can help them navigate these issues that will

---

[50] Ibid.

[51] Ibid.

undoubtedly need to be addressed in the early days and weeks of separation.

The counselees must sign a release or verbally authorize the Mediator to talk with the counselors and the church. If the counselees have procured their own mediator, ask them to provide the mediator's name and phone number.

There are many issues to be settled regarding the basics of life during a separation. The Mediator's primary role is to assist the couple in developing a framework to enable two separate households to function while each person is focusing on counseling and soul care (1 Cor. 12:27-28). The Mediator will work with the husband and wife regarding the arrangements to be made for the home's proper care and management during a protracted separation. The Mediator assists the couple by acting as the go-between and or relays information, questions, or concerns between the husband and wife, assists in scheduling child visitation, any child support to be paid, the payment of household bills, mowing the grass, paying for the counseling services, etc.

Before each week's counseling session, the counselor and the mediator should talk to secure accurate information about what has been going on with the counselee since the last meeting. Ask about the counselee's contact with their spouse, any children, issues over finances, the proper care of the home, or other concerns to address these in the counseling session. This provides the counselors with a more accurate picture of what is happening away from the counseling office.

Mentors

We hope that the church will recommend a couple of individuals to walk alongside our counselees as they receive biblical counseling in the weeks and months ahead. When some form of abuse is involved, we encourage a close working relationship with designated, spiritually mature people from the church to function as mentors and assistant disciplers to the counselors (Titus 2). The mentors need not be married to each other but should be able to work well together and have strong marriages of their own and a solid grasp of the Word of God. Ideally, the mentors will have had some biblical counseling training or be willing to be coached by us. Having people available for accountability and mentoring will be a tremendous benefit for the counselee's, the church, and the counselors.

The mentoring couple will provide accountability and be involved in the day-to-day and week-to-week lives of the abuser and the victim. When possible, they will accompany each to their weekly counseling sessions and have personal and online interaction with them when necessary. The mentors are not "counselors," but they will assist in the counseling process by reinforcing the counseling sessions' biblical principles throughout the week. The mentors will keep the rest of the team informed of the couple's progress in biblical counseling. While it is not ideal, one of the mentors may also act as the mediator between the husband and wife, if necessary.

Together, we will comprise the counseling team, working closely with the church to help the couple in the process of biblical change.

Common Errors Made When Evaluating Abuse

Open your mouth for the mute, for the rights of all the unfortunate. Open your mouth, judge righteously, and defend the rights of the afflicted and needy. Prov. 31:8-9

The Christian church has an obligation to protect those who are oppressed and in danger (Jas. 4:17; Prov. 24:11-12). Many churches take the issue of oppression and abuse in marriage very seriously. They listen carefully to the victims' complaints, do a thorough investigation, and provide protection, support, and counseling to the individuals and their families (Prov. 18:13,15,17).

However, some pitfalls need to be avoided if care is to be successful when abuse is present. We offer some common errors that we have encountered in our work with those affected by domestic abuse and committed by those helping the couple through this challenging time.

"Believe the Victim"

The statement "believe the victim" is often uttered by domestic violence counselors. We agree that the victim must be heard, and the allegations are taken seriously (Jn. 8:59, 10:39; Acts 9:25). However, it is crucial that both people are interviewed when there is an allegation of abuse. Scripture says,

He who gives an answer before he hears, it is folly and shame to him. Proverbs 18:13

The mind of the prudent acquires knowledge, And the ear of the wise seeks knowledge. Proverbs 18:15

The first to plead his case seems right, until another comes and examines him. Proverbs 18:17

When only one side of the story is heard, there is a risk of coming to the wrong conclusion about the problem and its origin. Biblical counselor Jim Newheiser points out that there are cases where accusations of abuse are false and are made to seek revenge or control (Deut. 19:16). Someone wrongly accused of abuse can lose their reputation, livelihood, be convicted of a crime they did not commit, and lose contact with their children.[52] Thus, it is important to establish a pattern of habitual, excessive, and destructive sinful behaviors (Deut. 19:15).

Allegations of domestic abuse are complicated because abuse typically happens in isolation when there are no witnesses. Therefore, some consider it he-said-she-said situation. For this reason, a complete and thorough investigation should be done by a biblical counselor with experience in domestic violence counseling who can assist the church leadership in assessing the situation (Deut. 19:18a). This will help avoid other pitfalls mentioned in this section. An important caveat when investigating an abuse allegation is that a wife may not initially reveal the full extent of the abuse she endures. She may only tell the counselor or pastor fragments of the abuse because she is scared. Once she knows you are safe and take her allegations seriously, she may disclose much more, and often the most severe aspects of the abuse. The wife should never be forced to detail the abuse's specifics in her husband's presence. This is <u>very</u> dangerous when the couple is still living together. It

---

[52] Jim Newheiser, *Helping Churches to Handle Cases of Abuse,* Light in the Darkness, ACBC Annual Conference, 2018.

puts her at tremendous risk of harm if she has to go home with him.

Blaming the Victim

Another pitfall occurs when the victim is blamed for the treatment he or she is receiving. It is important to remember that abuse must be defined by the behaviors of the abuser and not by the reactions or responses of the victim. While there may be genuine failures on the part of the victim, they do not justify abusive or oppressive treatment.

Gert never missed an opportunity to remind Shawn what a failure he was as a Christian man and husband. Shawn never quite measured up to her idea of a husband or the lowest standard of being a Christian man. Daily she would list the things he did and shouldn't have done or something he didn't do that he should have done. Gert kept the calendar for the family. She controlled the home, the finances, the discipline of their twin teenage daughters, and social life. He was not allowed to make a decision without consulting her.

Shawn continued to try and please his wife, apologizing and seeking her forgiveness, even when he did nothing wrong. Gert demanded that he listen to long diatribes of his inadequacies as a husband and father. If he left the house to escape her rantings, she would accuse him of avoiding her. If he stayed, he was not allowed to express his perspective on the matter.

Shawn sought the help of a man in the church who told him he was wrong for avoiding Gert when she was angry. He was to live with her in an understanding way (I Peter 3:7). He was told to examine himself and repent of the behaviors she brought to his attention. Shawn was further beaten down and depressed as he left that discussion.

Responses like those in the above vignette will confirm in the victim's mind that the things their spouse says about them are true. A husband likely has his wife well-groomed to accept his accusations and manipulations as the truth.

When the wife is the abuser, she has often been dominating the relationship for so long that the husband has abandoned his God-given leadership role.

The majority of the abused or oppressed people we meet are usually more than willing to admit they have sinned in the marriage. They will readily agree that they have issues of the heart that need work, and many victims say that they are partially at fault for how they are being treated. Even when the victim has sin issues to be addressed, it is *never* appropriate for the abuser to take physical or verbal vengeance against them (Rom. 12:17-18).

Focusing on the Victims' Responses (Resistance)

Resistance to oppressive or abusive treatment is the victim's attempt to confront their abuser's sin and maintain their sanity amid the ongoing use of abuse tactics. The victim can be broken down physically and emotionally, or so confused that they wonder if *they* are the abuser (as their spouse says they are) or just crazy. Many victims describe being mocked or diminished by their spouses as they attempt to be understood.

Their sinful responses (resistance) often result after repeated attempts to be heard have been ignored. These responses may or may not be sinful. The reactions to abusive treatment might include bitterness, resentment, hostility, and verbal retaliation. They can also escalate to pushing, shoving, hitting, and even, in very extreme cases, murder.

Chang was controlling and manipulative. He would get angry when Tina wanted to spend time with a girlfriend and guilt her to stay home. Tina responded by complaining and arguing with Chang and would go out anyway. Chang would escalate by threatening to take away the car keys to call her friend and tell her to "get lost."

Tina responded by sneaking out of the house to meet her friend for lunch under the guise of going to the store.

When Chang learned she had snuck a meeting with her friend, he angrily confronted her, and a screaming match ensued. He warned her this kind of thing would not be tolerated. He emphasized his words by punching his fist into the palm of this other hand.

Tina threatened to call the police or leave home, grabbed her cell phone and purse, and started for the door. Chang blocked the doorway and fought her for her cell phone. Tina escaped through the back door after scratching Chang's face. When the couple went to the pastor for counseling, Tina was chastised for not submitting to Chang's authority, lying to him about her secret lunch, and scratching him. Chang was told to allow his wife to have an occasional lunch out with a friend.

While these sins must be addressed in the counseling process, focusing on the victim's reactions, instead of the abuse that provokes (triggers) the response, can frequently be a pitfall. We have noted that, unfortunately, in the church, there tends to be a greater focus on the victim's responses than on the abuse itself. The victim is blamed, criticized, rebuked, and admonished for their (possibly sinful) response, while the abuser's behavior is minimized. This is a simplistic, shallow solution that doesn't confront the real issue: the abuser's heart.

Siding with the Abuser

As has been previously stated, when an allegation of abuse is made, somebody must investigate the matter. While the victim's motive in the disclosure is to seek help, the abuser's reason is to convince you that their spouse is wrong. It is very common for the abusive spouse to employ various manipulative tactics to influence the church or counselor and garner support. They will do this by criticizing and blaming their spouse. Most abusers attack, fault find, mind read, present records of wrongs, and tell elaborate stories to convince the hearer that there is little or no foundation to the accusations and redirect attention onto their spouse. Though this seems odd, it is not uncommon for the abuser to be believed despite their aggressive and hostile rhetoric. The victim is blamed for the difficulties in the home. Ironically, in abuse citations, the viler the narrative is against the victim, the more it is believed.

We have seen too many situations where the abuser successfully persuades significant others in the couple's lives (counselors, pastors, family) that their spouse is at fault after abusive behaviors are exposed. The abusive party often makes friends with key people in the church who only have a narrow view of their character. Perhaps they are valued Sunday school teachers, youth leaders, women's ministry leaders, or seminary students, and no one sees the side of them that is visible in the home. Sadly, we have seen the church body befriend and support the abuser and effectively "take his or her side." This is one of many reasons we recommend using a team approach for domestic abuse counseling (Prov. 11:14, 15:22, 24:6). We urge you to be cautious and wise when interviewing a spouse who has been accused of being abusive.

Minimizing the Abuse

Unfortunately, many do not understand the dynamics of emotional and verbal abuse and minimize abusive behaviors. Lack of understanding is among the top common complaints gathered from women who are experiencing non-physical abuse. Those we have counseled have been told the following things by those to whom they have gone for help:

- Everyone's definition of verbal or emotional abuse is different.
- Perhaps you are just overly sensitive.
- Many people have bad times in marriage; it'll get better over time.
- It's not that bad; at least he's not beating you up.
- Everyone has troubles; maybe it was just a bad day.
- God wants you to stay in the marriage and make it work.
- God wants you to learn to suffer well.

Debi Pryde and Robert Needham say the following regarding minimizing abuse of women:

> Pastors and other counselors face a great danger of contributing to a real catastrophe, as well as becoming guilty of serious biblical error, by telling an abused wife to go back to her husband and "suffer for Jesus' sake." Such counselors often use 1 Peter 3:1 – 6 as their justification for such counsel, failing to distinguish between a difficult and/or unbelieving husband, and one who is terrorizing a family.[53]

We would add that much of their statement applies to the abuse of men as well. We have seen women who horribly emotionally and verbally abuse their husbands. Women can indeed terrorize their husbands and their families by their words and deeds. The men are often embarrassed and confide abuse with difficulty.

---

[53] Debi Pryde, & Robert Needham, *A Biblical Perspective of What to do When You Are Abused by Your Husband,* 9.

To tell a man to "live with your wife in an understanding way (1 Pet. 3:7-8) is, of course, biblical. However, to use it to minimize a wife's abusive behavior is not helpful. To minimize a husband's concerns and complaints is harmful to them and the rest of the family. The abused men we have worked with will agree that it is their role to lead their wives, and they are incredibly frustrated with the barrage of criticism and lack of cooperation they receive from their wives.

We believe God uses our suffering to make us more like Christ (Rom. 8:28, 29). We must add that both Julie and I (Bill) firmly believe that God intends for marriage to be a lifelong covenant between a man and a woman. However, these biblical truths do not justify giving bad counsel that keeps a victim in an abusive situation and fails to hold the perpetrator accountable for their actions (Ps. 82:4). This highlights the need for thorough data gathering involving both individuals as part of the counseling process.

Offering Misguided Counsel

Many victims are given simplistic and even dangerous counsel. Some of the commonly offered opinions and suggestions given to a wife are:

- Make him feel special.
- Commit to praying for him.
- Learn to submit more.
- Be willing to have more sex.
- That's just how men are!
- Talk to him about how his actions and behavior affect you (especially if it is emotional or verbal abuse).

- Be more open; tell him how you feel.
- Learn to listen more.
- Be sensitive to his stress/needs.
- Change the home atmosphere.
- Be patient.
- Be more loving.

Men who are victims of abuse are also offered counsel that does not address the heart of the problem. They are told:

- To live with their wife in an understanding way.
- To stop reacting to their wife and be a godly example.
- To accept that their wives can be hormonal.
- To not emotionally shut off from your wife.
- To stop avoiding your wife.
- To ask what God is teaching you.
- To listen to the concerns of your wife.
- To stop abusing your wife by walking away or by getting angry.

To be clear, many of these recommendations are just fine in a normal, healthy marriage. The couple will be taught how to implement some of them in the reconciliation and reunification phases of counseling. However, when abuse is active and ongoing, understand that the abused spouse has most likely tried many of those suggestions. More importantly, these things don't stop the abuse. *The victim is not the problem.* Placing the responsibility on *them* to adapt and change to alter their spouse's abusive actions is unbiblical (Rom. 16:18). This unwittingly contributes to and reinforces their abuser's false beliefs and furthers their determination that the victim accepts the blame for their actions. The victim could do it all "right," and the abusive behaviors will continue because abuse is a heart issue centering on the use of various tactics to enforce power and control over another person.

We have found that those who abuse and profess to be Christians have become skillful at perverting the Bible to dominate and control their spouses (Lk. 16:15). Their confidence in their ability to understand the Bible is undermined and promotes tremendous self-doubt and confusion. They come to believe the lies spoken about them and doubt they can do anything right. They immediately feel guilt and shame when criticized.

Requiring Marriage Counseling

Marriage counseling is NOT the appropriate initial course of action in domestic oppression and other forms of domestic abuse/violence. **Abuse is not primarily a marriage issue**; it is an issue of the heart between the abuser and God and between the abused spouse and God.

It is pointless to try to deal with sin problems in the marriage relationship until the abuser is willing and (by God's grace) able to repent of *their own sins first* (Matt. 7:3 – 5). They have convinced themselves (and others) that their behaviors are a direct result of other people in their life who have not dealt with them as they "deserve." If the sinful behavior is considered a marriage problem before the issues of coercive power and control are addressed, this will contribute to the abuser's self-deception.

Counselor Brad Hambrick says,

To address 'marital issues' in an abusive context is a form of minimizing the abuse... Counseling in abusive situations should not be marriage counseling. Both spouses should be counseled separately until they can both consistently acknowledge that the abusive or neglectful actions are the predominant issue.[54]

Pastor Chris Moles agrees that domestic violence is a heart problem and not a marriage problem. He says,

Marriage-focused solutions may do more harm than good in cases of domestic violence... Most professionals believe that marriage counseling endangers the victim through often unintended, but real consequences.[55]

At some point, marriage counseling will be needed, but not until the violence or oppression has been thoroughly and biblically addressed, and each spouse has individually shown the fruit of repentance and heart change toward God.

Giving Grace Instead of Correction

I (Julie) was taught that if you do not believe someone when they tell you something, you call them a liar, even when there is a great reason to be skeptical. People who abuse are often very cunning and proficient in deception. They seize the opportunity to manipulate the helper with charm further to form bonds with their counselor. Their explanations sound very reasonable; they admit to wrongdoing, "getting angry" or "losing their temper," and they "don't see" what they have been doing as "abuse" or as a pattern of behavior that is grievously sinful and harmful.

---

[54] Brad Hambrick, *Self-Centered Spouse,* 23.

[55] Chris Moles, *The Heart of Domestic Abuse,* 15.

They perceive niceness as a weakness and will take advantage of the grace given to them. These tactics (lies, manipulation, a general admission of wrongdoing) are often used during the evaluation, especially when the abusive person wants to convince the counselor of their repentance.

Christians desire to give grace when a person says they have repented. We want to believe them; we want to believe they have changed or that they haven't committed those sinful acts in the first place, but this is a grave error. We recommend giving more attention to what they have done or *doing* rather than what they are *saying* because their words alone are not trustworthy (Lk. 6:43-45; Gal. 5:16-18; Matt. 15:11, 18-19).

Rushing Reunification

There are occasions when a couple is separated because the abuse is severe enough to concern the victim's physical, emotional, and mental safety (Ps. 140:12; Isa. 1:17). As previously stated, it takes time for the abuser first to recognize their sinful attitudes of the heart and then begin the change of thoughts, beliefs, and desires that have been a part of his or her life for many years. In most cases, these are lifelong issues, and it is unrealistic to expect or anticipate change in a week, a month, or even several months (although miraculous things do happen). The victim must also experience heart change. He or she has learned to accommodate their spouse's sinful behavior and must learn new and biblical ways to respond to them. These changes also take time.

Rushing reunification can derail the counselee's repentance and meaningful progress. This is because reunification focuses on the marriage and each other and takes the focus off of personal repentance and off living to glorify God. In some situations, rushing reunification places one of them in danger.

Mateo and Dana were separated after it was discovered that Mateo was emotionally abusing his wife. They had been separated and in counseling for several months, and Mateo appeared to be making progress in addressing his abusive heart. When the church noticed his improvement in counseling, Dana was pressured to allow Mateo to come home.

When they met with their counselors, Mateo read a long letter that detailed his sin against Dana and told her he had changed. He promised that his previous sinful actions of control and abusive anger, and ungodly words toward her were in the past. Mateo was sure of his repentance, that he was a changed person, that God had convicted him of his sin, and that he would never return to those behaviors again. His confession was accompanied by tears and pleading. He repeatedly pledged his undying love for her and begged her to let him come home. Dana chose to "give him the benefit of the doubt," and Mateo moved back home. Unfortunately, shortly after, their reunification resumed his abusive talk and renewed his threats of physical violence.

Sadly, the sinful responses of some of our counselee's have verified this to be accurate. Be alert to attempts by the abuser to manipulate and gain favor apart from genuine change. Behaviors are the evidence of a changed heart, and repentant actions should be demonstrated over a long enough time period to validate their genuineness (Gal. 5: 22-24). We have a responsibility to the victim to ensure (as much as anyone can) that their spouse will not resume abusive patterns of behavior once reconciliation and reunification have taken place.

Repentance

One Way Forward

Repentance is a crucial stop on *The Roadmap.* Both husband and wife must understand that there is only one way forward in a marriage that has been affected by abuse. The way forward includes the abusive person repenting of the sin that has entangled them, and the spouse repenting of the sinful attitudes and responses that have developed as a result (Heb. 12:1,15). Without repentance, there will be no genuine change (Eph. 4:22-24; Rom. 12:1-2).

In a counseling situation, both victims and oppressors need to understand that domestic violence is about power and control. We want every pastor and counselor to know that *every* abuse case will contain power and control, which is maintained by manipulation and anger. Julie and I address these issues individually with the victim and the abuser at the beginning of our counseling relationships. It is imperative to understand how to identify and address these primary components of domestic oppression and domestic violence in all its forms.

"Abusive men come from every walk of life, every income bracket, and every race and culture. With rare exceptions, friends, family, and business associates never guess or suspect wife abuse by the abuser's behavior in their presence."[56]As unfortunate as this truth is, it is no surprise

---

[56] Debi Pryde, & Robert Needham, *A Biblical Perspective of What to do When You Are Abused by Your Husband,* 16.

to God, and He does not overlook it. As he says in Psalm 11:4-5, *"Those who love violence he hates with a passion."* Men who abuse, twist their theology, and are deceived in their thinking about sin.

The reality is that the heart of an abuser is focused on himself. He is not thinking of God, his wife, or his children. He is focused on gaining and maintaining **power** and **control** over his victim. He typically uses **anger** and manipulation to get and keep that power and control. His actions are intended to dominate and control every aspect of his victim's life by frightening and manipulating her into obedience and submission to his desires.

> The abuser's ultimate goal is to get his emotional and physical desires met. He aims to selfishly make use of his partner to meet those needs. Most abusers are afraid their desires will not be fulfilled through a normal, healthy relationship. Fear motivates them to use abuse to ensure that their desires will be met.[57]

Abusers are brutes who are judgmental of sinners and who use another person's sins to justify their desires to control as well as their violent and emotional abuse (Luke 18: 9-14). The reason they use power, control, and anger is to get what they want. They are selfish, and they are desperate. They want to change their environment to avoid looking into their own heart motives. They are afraid because, in truth, their pretend kingdom is falling apart, and

---

[56] Justin Holcomb & Lindsay Holcomb, *Is It My Fault? Hope and Healing for Those Suffering Domestic Violence*, 58.

another ruler is in town. The challenge for the counselor is to continue to exhibit the fruits of God's Spirit and to not fall into the trap of being judgmental and critical.

Power

Power is a *desire* of his heart. There is much talk these days about young people and their sense of entitlement, and that may be true, but it is also prevalent in the hearts and minds of many men who abuse their wives. This is, unfortunately, all too true of men who call themselves Christian. These external and apparent shows of force are simplistic, self-serving, and ungodly.

The abuser thinks and believes: I am in charge, I am the head of my wife, I have a right to be respected, she is inferior to me, I must make all the decisions. The results of these thoughts, beliefs, and desires are revealed as the abuser demeans, degrades, and shames his wife. He uses violence or threats of violence to get her in line, uses the children to get her to cooperate, and uses anger to frighten her into submission.

The notion that "might-makes-right" or "top-down leadership" is only appropriate when properly placing God into the equation. The Psalmist notes in Psalm 50:1, *"The Mighty One, God, the Lord, has spoken, and summoned the earth from the rising of the sun to its setting,"* and in Psalm 24:1-2, *"The earth is the Lord's, and all it contains the world, and those who dwell in it. For He has founded it upon the seas And established it upon the rivers."*

God has the authority and the power to create the heavens and the earth (Gen. 1:1). However, the power men are to wield, with the power of God's Holy Spirit, is described for us in Paul's writings, and it is a power very different from the kind of power wielded by violent, abusive men. Some examples are:

Empowered to live self-controlled lives:

> *For the grace of God has appeared, bringing salvation to all men, instructing us to deny ungodliness and worldly desires and to live sensibly, righteously and godly in the present age.* Titus 2:11-12

Empowered to admit their own sin:

> *But the tax collector, standing some distance away, was even unwilling to lift up his eyes to heaven, but was beating his breast, saying, 'God, be merciful to me, the sinner!'* Luke 18:13

Empowered to stand firm under trials:

> *Blessed is a man who perseveres under trial; for once he has been approved, he will receive the crown of life which the Lord has promised to those who love Him.* James 1:12

Empowered to be content in weakness for the sake of Christ:

> *Therefore I am well content with weaknesses, with insults, with distresses, with persecutions, with difficulties, for Christ's sake; for when I am weak, then I am strong.* 2 Corinthians 12:10

Empowered to face plenty and hunger:

> *I know how to get along with humble means, and I also know how to live in prosperity; in any and every circumstance I have learned the secret of being filled*

and going hungry, both of having abundance and suffering need. Philippians 4:12

Control

Abusive people desire to control every facet of the relationship. They want to control their spouse's dialogue, actions, thoughts, and behaviors by using tactics found on the Power and Control Wheel. Control is another aspect of the sinful heart.

The abusive person believes they have a biblical right to this control. A husband might claim Eph 5:23a as his right to control his wife as her "head." The abuser thinks and believes: I must monitor my spouse's friendships and relationships, I must control all the spending, I must manage how my wife spends her time when I am away, I must determine how my wife and children dress, how much my spouse eats and sleeps.

They also want to control the frequency and expression of their sexual intimacy. God has authorized mankind to be in control under his divine sovereignty. He commands us to demonstrate control or dominion over the earth (Gen 2:15, Gen 1:26-28). People are to act as God's representatives and care for the earth in ways that reflect his character. This means we are to take care of it as stewards waiting for the Owner to return (Ps.24:1). God also commands us to be self-controlled, not controlling others (Prov.25:28; Gal. 5:22-23; 2 Tim. 1:7; Titus 1:8). God is ultimately in control of everything. *"Our God is in the heavens, and he does all that he pleases"* Psalm 115:3. God's sovereignty is exercised for our good and his glory. This is contrasted with the controlling desires of an abusive person who has only their interests at heart. Some examples are:

Control over our tongues

> *And the tongue is a fire, a world of unrighteousness. The tongue is set among our members, staining the whole body, setting on fire the entire course of life, and set on fire by hell.* James 3:6

Control over our temper

> *"You have heard that it was said to those of old, 'You shall not murder; and whoever murders will be liable to judgment.' But I say to you that everyone who is angry with his brother will be liable to judgment; whoever insults his brother will be liable to the council; and whoever says, 'You fool!' will be liable to the hell of fire.* Matt. 5: 21-22 (ESV)

Control over our thoughts

> *Put to death therefore what is earthly in you: sexual immorality, impurity, passion, evil desire, and covetousness, which is idolatry. On account of these the wrath of God is coming. In these you too once walked, when you were living in them. But now you must put them all away: anger, wrath, malice, slander, and obscene talk from your mouth. Do not lie to one another, seeing that you have put off the old self with its practices ...* Colossians 3:5-9 (ESV)

Control over our actions/body

> *...that each of you should learn to control your own body in a way that is holy and honorable.* 1 Thess. 4:4 (NIV)

Control over our emotions

> *What causes quarrels and what causes fights among you? Is it not this, that your passions are at war within you?* James 4:1 (ESV)

Anger

Anger arises as the abuser tries to manage their small world in a way that is fitting to their desires. When those desires are not met, abusive people experience frustration that's often expressed in sinful, ungodly, destructive, and harmful ways (Prov. 14:12). This anger response is yet another tactic used by a person to intimidate their spouse. It creates fear to get their self-centered desires fulfilled. Violent anger harms others, hurts those near the abuser, and it destroys relationships. *"An angry man stirs up dissension, and a hot-tempered one commits many sins"* Proverbs 29:22.

When enraged, an abusive person may hit, slap, ridicule, have an unpredictable and explosive temper, threaten, intimidate, coerce, and destroy property. However, it is essential to understand that they may internalize the violence besides the more visible expressions of anger. Instead of blowing up, they may sulk, engage in self-pity, and resort to sarcasm, biting humor, or manipulative crying.[58]

However, not all anger is expressed in violent outbursts, yelling, hitting, or breaking things. It is also visible through closing off communications, muttering, feeding bitterness, resenting others, clamming up, and murmuring. *"They murmured in their tents and did not obey the voice of the Lord"* Psalm 106:25. Whether the anger is expressed in violence or withdrawal, ungodly anger is in the abuser's heart. The

---

[58] Debi Pryde & Robert Needham, *A Biblical Perspective of What to do When You Are Abused by Your Husband,* 47-48.

abuser's sinful words and actions are the revelations of what is in his heart.

> And He [Jesus]was saying, "That which proceeds out of the man, that is what defiles the man. For from within, out of the heart of men, proceed the evil thoughts, fornications, thefts, murders, adulteries, deeds of coveting and wickedness, as well as deceit, sensuality, envy, slander, pride and foolishness. All these evil things proceed from within and defile the man." Mark 7: 20 – 23)

Unwilling to take responsibility for their sinful anger or self-idolatry, such people blame and express their anger in violent rages or physical and emotional withdrawal. Wickedness, covetousness, pride, foolishness, all these things and more, are lurking in the abuser's heart, feeding his thoughts, beliefs, and desires. James 4:1-3 drives the point home.

> What is the source of quarrels and conflicts among you? Is not the source your pleasures that wage war in your members? You lust and do not have; so you commit murder. You are envious and cannot obtain; so you fight and quarrel. You do not have because you do not ask. You ask and do not receive, because you ask with wrong motives, so that you may spend it on your pleasures. Jas. 4:1-3

James reveals that the fighting and disagreements come from within, a desire for pleasure that wars in the heart. When a person's heart is filled with such lusts (v2) as "I want," "I need," "I deserve," sinful anger and all its manifestations are lurking at the door.

Often rights being claimed are "perceived" and not biblical. These various "rights" are thought to be typical, expected, and sometimes demanded in our western culture. When confronted with God's word on "our rights," there is an anticipated pushback I (Bill) have found when referring to the violent abuser for clarification from God's word of truth.

As previously stated, our primary goal in this situation is to counsel people on how to bring God glory through personal transformation leading to marital reconciliation. At Reigning Grace Counseling Center, we do **not** encourage divorce. We believe the divorce decision should remain between the victim and her church leaders. Whenever possible, our goal is always biblical reconciliation, even in cases of domestic oppression and violence. The counselee is aware that this counseling process is a long journey with no specific time limit and can take a year or more.

Repenting from the Heart of Abuse

Matthew 7:16-20 says,

> *You will know them by their fruits. Grapes are not gathered from thorn bushes nor figs from thistles, are they? So every good tree bears good fruit, but the bad tree bears bad fruit. A good tree cannot produce bad fruit, nor can a bad tree produce good fruit. Every tree that does not bear good fruit is cut down and thrown into the fire. So then, you will know them by their fruits.*

We use a diagram of the tree to personalize the evidence of the abuse and tactics to manipulate his wife to meet his own selfish wants and perceived needs. This is in contrast to sacrificial love and servant leadership (Jn. 13:1-6). He must see how his fruit is evidence he has made his wife an idol in the attempt to get from her what only God can give him.

He is deceived in his own heart (Jer. 17:9). If he admits to his sin, it is usually as vague as is the fruit he places on his tree. He makes statements such as, "I lost my temper," "I had an emotional reaction," "I spoke out of hand," or "I was insensitive to my wife." He should instead state specific behavioral sins such as "I punched a hole in the sheetrock," "I (pushed) shoved my wife," "I threw (blank) at the window and smashed it." In addition to the minimization or outright denial of his violence, he unapologetically blames his wife for his sin(s) (Prov. 28:13). I (Bill) need them to make the connection between their behavior and power and control over their spouse and their use of anger to achieve their selfish goals.

Once he details his sin, he is encouraged to recognize his sins' seriousness and corrosive effects on his spouse. The fruit on his tree needs to include the use of physical violence. This abuse may not be a direct physical assault like punching or hitting, but just as intimidating and controlling is his use of physical force by pushing, physically restraining, grabbing, pinching, slapping, or blocking his wife from escaping. As his sinful heart is revealed, he will repeatedly say, "You (the counselor) don't understand."

"I Don't Understand."

This is commonly one of the first statements an abuser will make. He uses this rationale as a kind of humble acknowledgment of failure on his part. He quickly proceeds to subtly blame his wife for not communicating her needs, wants, or concerns adequately. He will say, "Now that I know she is unhappy, I can make adjustments and make the home life better for her." This is manipulation.

Our Lord calls husbands to live with their wives in an understanding way (1 Pet. 3:7), and by his own admission, he does not understand. This initial tactic is useful for me as the biblical counselor when I'm later informing him of the need for counseling. In my experience, I might add that the "I don't get it" or "I don't understand" is frequently stated many times. This admission of disbelief and confusion allows me to use his own words to validate the need for ongoing biblical counseling.

"My Wife is Just Like This."

This plea is intended to divide me from my female co-counselor and to get me to acknowledge what he notes as stereotypical male-female differences. When he tells me his wife "is just like this," or "just like that," I ask him, "Like what?" Many of the men I counsel will now open up about her lack of submission, their frequent arguing, his and her yelling, her poor parenting, as well as her lack of sexual responsiveness. They will tell me how they've taken the high road and listened, ". . .but she keeps pushing, and I had to do something. She pushed my buttons, and so what is a guy to do?" These men avert responsibility and quickly add that the conflicts are blown out of proportion by their wife's emotional moodiness. I've actually heard several of my counselees say, "You know, like all women." These abusive men make frequent use of the words "she" and "her" as they talk about their wives. This is another way the men stereotype and denigrate their wives.

I do not join him in his stereotyped description, nor do I take sides. I will instead acknowledge his view of the issues and then attempt to redirect him to recognize how he has contributed to some of the issues (1 Jn. 1:5). I will make a mental note, but not say at this time, that he is giving me a substantial reason for the need for ongoing biblical counseling and for considering separation (after consultation with his pastor and the rest of the counseling team).

"Being Separated from My Wife is Unbiblical."

The majority of the married couples we see at Reigning Grace are already separated by the time we see them. Either their church has directed the wife to leave for her safety or has left on her own accord. In the initial meeting, the husband will make the statement, "Being separated from my wife is unbiblical." He will cite Mark 10:9 as evidence that his wife should come back home. I will clarify that the immediate need is to protect his wife while gathering data and creating a counseling plan. This plea also attempts to place the "blame" for the separation on the counseling team and his wife.

Many men will challenge me to find a Scripture that supports this separation. I will take the husband to Proverbs 27:12 *The prudent see danger and take cover; but the simple keep going and pay the penalty.* I want him to understand that we have an obligation to protect his wife from harm (Prov. 22:3; 14:16). We also look at Titus 2: 2-4, and I help him see how his behaviors are not in line with these instructions for godly men. Most abusive men rapidly leave this tactic to avoid looking at their own sin. If the husband disagrees that he has violated a number of these "to be" statements, I will tell him his wife is following Matthew 18:15-18, and we are the two or three witnesses who are hearing these facts. We are obligated biblically to get a fuller understanding of the facts. Thus, he is here, and she is protected. He needs to comprehend that trust has been broken. For him to earn her trust, he must exhibit repentance by showing consistent actions over time.

"My Pastor and All My Friends Agree with Me."

Many abusive men use "others" to garner support for their selfish demands. They use relationships with their pastor, friends, church members, social media contacts for recognition, approval, and support.

I have had men contact distant relatives of their wife, give them their side of the story, and ask those relatives to call their wife and convince her to come home or retract her accusations of abuse. Some men bring an unannounced friend or pastor who is often a co-conspirator to one or more initial sessions. This person is brought along to align with the abuser. This tactic often backfires when the friend or pastor hears the *complete story*. "The first to state his case seems right until another comes forward and examines him," Proverbs 18:17. This should be seen as an opportunity to educate his friend and bring his pastor into the counseling team.

"You Need to Hear My Side of the Story..."

It is common for husbands to express their belief that no one listens to them, that others are only listening to his wife, and that no one cares about him or cares to listen to his side of the story. There is a need for me to listen and allow him to voice his perspective on the situation.

It is likely true that the couple has been brimming with resentments and keeping records of wrongs over the years. The husband sharing his side of the story sometimes reduces some of his defensiveness, and again, I can use this information to confirm why they may need to be apart during this phase of the counseling process.

He will want to keep focusing on the problems between him and his wife. He will request marriage counseling. The abusive husband wants power and control over his wife. He wants her to be different, and he uses anger in an attempt to achieve both of those sinful desires of his heart. He will deny HE is the problem. You needn't attempt to clarify his confusion. If he understood God's will in this relationship, he'd be doing it by now. Allow his confusion to be a catalyst for his seeking counsel to fix the problem in his heart.

The counseling goal is to bring to light the abuser's heart motives to exert power over another and control another, and we point him back to his own heart motives. The counselor can refer the husband to Jeremiah 17:9 or Proverbs 14:12, *"There is a way that seems right to a man, but its end is the way of death"* to confirm that though his way of managing his home and leading his family *seemed* right to him, it leads to sin and destruction. He *does* what seems right to him in his own eyes, and it has left devastating results. God's ways are undoubtedly different from man's ways (Isa. 55:8-9), and the need is for biblical repentance and not a mere acknowledgment.

It is critical to address heart issues rather than only focusing on the actions of abuse. In a secular treatment model, he would be referred to a secular counselor. The focus would be on providing therapy for each of the triggers or actions of abuse. He would likely be sent to a communication course, anger management, or a batterer's class. The goal is moral reform to help him manage his feelings and emotions. These issues are often wrongly considered to be the reason a person is abusive. Such courses may not be harmful, but they will not address the heart of the problem. Look at what Matthew 12: 43 – 45 says about moral reform apart from heart change.

> *Now when the unclean spirit goes out of a man, it passes through waterless places seeking rest, and does not find it. Then it says, 'I will return to my house from which I came'; and when it comes, it finds it unoccupied, swept, and put in order. Then it goes and takes along with it seven other spirits more wicked than itself, and they go in and live there, and the last state of that man becomes worse than the first. That is the way it will also be with this evil generation.*

We are not suggesting that abusive behavior can be blamed on demons or unclean spirits. What we are saying is that we must consider what a behavioristic or therapeutic approach accomplishes. The person who abuses their spouse will learn how to change their behaviors and achieve moral reform through cognitive behavioral therapy or a twelve-step program. However, unless their heart is changed (repentance), their abusive behaviors will likely return (Lk. 6:45).

The tree illustration reveals that the heart must get right with God before significant life changes occur. The motive of his or her heart must change from the worship of self to glorifying God. Therefore, addressing only the sinful words and actions of an abuser will, in the long term, be ineffective.

The Theology of Biblical Repentance

There are many questions regarding repentance and how to know when a person has genuinely repented. Repentance is critical in overcoming any manner of sin. The root of the word repentance is a change of mind, but that is not all that comprises this essential aspect of change. The way to determine what repentance is is by its usage. True biblical repentance is a response to sin found in the use of at least three different words that each express a different aspect of this biblical command. All three components must be present to be the fruit of true repentance in a person's life.

For a person to repent of abusing their spouse, they must first recognize their thoughts, beliefs, desires, and behaviors as sinful. We use the Word of God to show our counselees that their haughty (Prov. 21:24), arrogant (Prov. 15:12; Jer. 49:16), deceptive (Ps. 12:2), hypocritical (Matt. 15:7-9), and self-seeking (Deut. 8:11-15) actions are condemned in the Bible.

The first response of repentance is found in the Greek word metanoeo, which means a "change of mind" (to change one's mind for better, heartily to amend with abhorrence of one's past sins) (Matt. 3:2, Mk. 1:15).[59] When a person has a change of mind, there is an acknowledgment of sin. This is followed by confession, an admission, and understanding that how they treat their spouse is sinful. There is no justification or rationalization attached to sinning, no attempts to minimize or shift the responsibility for their abusive behaviors onto their spouse. The abusive spouse may or may not experience personal guilt over the sinful actions they have committed to this point. Typically, very early in the counseling process, the husband who

---

[59]*Metanoeō,*
Strongs 3340 hsttps://www.blueletterbible.org/lang/lexicon/lexicon.cfm?Strongs=G3340&t=KJV

has abused, dominated, and controlled his wife tells me (Bill) he has repented, he is changed, he loves his wife, and is now ready to return home. He validates his claims by telling me his actions, which supposedly "prove" that his repentance is real. He recounts his behavior changes that often have no connection to heart change. When confronted, he justifies his behavior and again proves that his motives are self-serving and not God-honoring.

Worldly Sorrow is Not Repentance

Peter was physically, verbally, and emotionally abusive toward his wife, Martha. He agreed to attend counseling because his wife and children left him. Initially, Peter made it clear he disagreed that he was "abusive," He rationalized and justified his behaviors and blamed her for their problems. Over six months of counseling, Peter understood his treatment of Martha was an abuse of authority and that his leadership was not loving. He was faithful to attend church, meet with a mentor in the church for Bible study, attend counseling, and do his homework. He appeared to be gaining in wisdom and knowledge. His counselor thought he was repentant, and Peter thought so too.

The pastor met with Peter and his counselor, and Peter made a case for why it would be best for him to return home to his wife and family. He said he had really learned his lesson and that for separation to continue was really a hardship on him. Peter said he needed his wife emotionally and sexually, and he thought his children needed their father in the home. He had accepted his consequences, but now it was time to move on and put this behind them. Peter said the counseling had been helpful, but he didn't think he needed to meet weekly anymore.

While verbally Peter accepted responsibility for his sin, there was little evidence he had truly repented. He did not hate his sin but felt bad about how it affected him and his family. His concern was about returning home and getting his needs met, and he was not thinking about how this would affect his wife and children.

Peter's understanding of his sin's consequences was only separation from his wife, not how his sin affected God or others. Peter thought that his wife should just forgive him and be willing to move on, to give grace and trust him again because he said he had changed. When the pastor and counselor disagreed with him and his plan for immediate reunification, Peter became angry and defended his position. He argued his points for going home and explained to the counseling team they were wrong. He told them they were insensitive, rigid, lacked understanding, were punishing him, and hurting his wife and family.

Sadly, Peter and Martha's story is typical; in fact, we commonly see it while counseling those caught up in some form of domestic abuse. Pastor John MacArthur says that worldly sorrow is "unsanctified remorse" and is focused on feelings of regret, fear, desperation, and how the exposure of their sin will affect them. He also says that worldly sorrow "has no redemptive capability. It is nothing more than the wounded pride of getting caught in a sin and having one's lusts go unfulfilled."[60]

So why do so many abusive people fail to change, and marriages end in divorce? There are a few common reasons that we have found in our work with domestic abuse couples. First, you must realize that the person who employs the tactics doesn't always see their actions as sinful. They don't believe there is anything to repent or change. Often, they slough it off as "It's just the way I am." Some maintain a sinful attitude of entitlement and refuse to change. They dig in, thinking, "He/She is not going to win." They believe their behaviors and words are justified.

In these cases, it is a matter for the church to take up discipline (Matt.18). Abuse is not about "hurt feelings" or someone's ideas about how a spouse should act; these are

---

[60]John MacArthur Study Bible, footnotes on 2 Corinthians 7:10

serious sin issues that demand repentance because GOD says so. When a person refuses to repent and chooses to live in ANY ongoing sin, the church must undertake discipline to enforce repentance and conformity to right living and change (1 Jn. 3:4-10; 1 Cor. 5:2; 2 Cor 5:17).

Genuine Repentance Brings Lasting Change

It is important to note that repentance is a manifestation of the life of Christ in a person. It is proof or evidence of salvation in a person's life. A repenting person is humble and aware of their own sins. They will ask God to change their thinking because they know their thoughts are selfish. The sinner has been cut deeply to the heart by the Spirit of God and or God's Word. They understand that their sin is grievous to the Lord. Because of accepting and understanding that spiritual reality, they no longer desire to participate in their sin. Repentance can come quickly, but in the case of a hard heart, it can take years of discipline or chastisement by the Lord. One thing is for sure: a regenerated Christian will repent. There will be no way for a person to live under the Holy Spirit's conviction and ministry without repenting.

The repentance we hope to see is a change of mind that supports an ongoing pattern of behavior change (Rom. 12:2). We look for behaviors that align themselves with thoughts, beliefs, and actions that flow from a worldview that aligns itself with those of God and His Holy Scriptures.

Repentance cannot stop with a change of mind because it is incomplete. There are plenty of situations in which a husband or wife confesses to abusively sinning against their spouse in the counselor or pastor's office, and nothing changes when they go back home. Things go back to normal, meaning the sinful tactics of ungodly power and control resume or new abusive behaviors take their place.

An excellent biblical example of incomplete repentance would be the Pharaoh as he dealt with Moses and the Israelites. Twice he admitted to Moses, "I have sinned against the Lord your God" (Ex. 9:27; 10:16). He acknowledged he sinned; he did not justify or rationalize or shift the blame, yet he did not repent. There were no other changes that accompanied his admission; in fact, he went right back to his behavior (Ex. 9:34-35; 10:20)!

King Saul had the same kind of incomplete repentance, and he did not cease pursuing David no matter how "sorry" he was (1 Sam.15:24, 24:17; 26:21). It is clear that just admitting sin does not equal repentance.

Recognition of sin leads to conviction by the Holy Spirit. The second critical aspect of repentance is metanolomai [to care afterwards, i.e., regret:—repent], and it means "change of heart" (Matt. 21:29, 32; Heb. 7:21). [61] In addition to admitting and confessing sin, there must be a heart change concerning the sin. What a person once loved and worshiped is now hated. The one who sinned against their spouse is grieved over their sin. They deeply regret their unloving, domineering leadership and abusive speech and actions. They desire to change because they understand they are not honoring God.

---

[61] metanolomai
https://www.blueletterbible.org/lang/lexicon/lexicon.cfm?Strongs=G3338&t=K
JV

There is no longer room in the heart for dominating and controlling their spouse; in fact, there is a growing hatred for everything that leads to that kind of behavior. They develop a holy hatred and emotional response of deep sorrow over their sin.

The first two aspects of repentance take place in the inner man or the heart. This is critical because as the heart is changed, the actions change, which leads us to the third aspect of biblical repentance which is a "change in the course of life" metanoia [a change of mind, as it appears to one who repents, of a purpose he has formed or of something he has done (Matt. 3:8; 9:13; Acts 20:21). [62]

Praise God that in Christ, *every abuser can change by the Holy Spirit's power* and by obeying the Word of God. Repentance and heart change are processes.

> "Bear[ing] fruits worthy of repentance" implies a process. Just as a tree does not produce fruit overnight, a Christian does not fully repent overnight. It is a lifelong process of making changes, and over time we will produce the fruit of the Spirit more consistently than the works of the flesh. [63]

Ephesians 4:22 – 24 begins to lay out the pattern for change:

> *...that, in reference to your former manner of life, you lay aside the old self, which is being corrupted in accordance with the lusts of deceit, and that you be renewed in the*

---

[62] metanoiahttps://www.blueletterbible.org/lang/lexicon/lexicon.cfm?Strongs=G3341&t=KJVStrongs 3341]

[63] Martin G. Collins basic Doctrines: Repentancehttps://www.bibletools.org/index.cfm/fuseaction/Topical.show/RTD/cgg/ID/5506/Bearing-Fruits-Worthy-Repentance.htm accessed 8/24/2020

spirit of your mind, and put on the new self, which in the likeness of God has been created in righteousness and holiness of the truth.

When Paul says, "put off" or "lay aside the old self," he speaks about more than just stopping offensive actions. Again, changes must go beyond behaviorism and go down to the heart. In verse 23, Paul says, *"...be renewed in the spirit of your mind..."* He says something similar in Romans 12:2:

> *And do not be conformed to this world, but be transformed by the renewing of your mind, so that you may prove what the will of God is, that which is good and acceptable and perfect.*

Here, the command is to be transformed by the renewing of your mind. To be transformed in this context comes from the Greek word *metamorphoo*, and it is the word from which we get metamorphosis.[64]

Every grade school child learns about metamorphosis by illustrating the caterpillar that turns into a butterfly. I (Julie) did not know that as the caterpillar spins the chrysalis, it is the beginning of his decomposition process. As that caterpillar remains inside the cocoon, it has spun, it decomposes, and when that process is complete, it is reduced to, in simple terms, caterpillar soup. The miraculous thing is that God takes that caterpillar soup and creates an entirely new and different insect out of it. The creature is a butterfly. The butterfly has absolutely no resemblance to the caterpillar in shape or form, and even parts of its DNA are different!

---

[64] *metamorphoo* https://www.blueletterbible.org/lang/lexicon/lexicon.cfm?Strongs=G3339&t=KJV

This kind of total transformation is what Paul refers to in Romans 12:2. This is possible for every single person who has experienced the new birth in Jesus Christ. What a hopeful truth for the Christian who abuses and for their spouse! This means they are capable of real and lasting change.

As their mind/heart is being changed through the Word of God and the Holy Spirit convicting them of sin, they will begin to see themselves and their spouse through the lens of Scripture. Their thoughts, beliefs, and desires will change. As God begins to transform their heart, they will respond with new and godly actions. They will desire to, as Ephesians 4:22 says, "put off" or get rid of the ungodly thoughts, beliefs, and desires of the heart that have been driving their sinful, abusive words and actions.

He or she will want to be more Christlike, and they will do battle with their flesh as they actively seek to "put on the new man," as verse 24 says, *that is created in righteousness and holiness of truth."* They will seek to honor and glorify God and not want to grieve the Holy Spirit (v 30).

A person desiring repentance recognizes their sinful ways are habitual. They need to develop new godly habits, so we make them accountable for their time in the Word of God, church attendance, what God is revealing to them from His Word, and how their thinking, motives, and behavior have changed as a result.

In the counseling process, we train our counselees to ask themselves questions intended to reveal the heart, such as: What are your beliefs about God? How does what you are doing exhibit a humble, broken spirit before God? How does what you just said or did show that you are humble before the sovereign God?

When they are repenting, the person is cooperating fully with the counseling plan and voices awareness of their self-righteousness, their attempts at manipulating others, and their anger. They are willing and eager to ask forgiveness from the injured party. They do not question the counseling plan.

When repentance is genuine, you will see all of this, and the change will be dramatic. *"Therefore, produce fruit that proves your repentance."* Matthew 3:8 (NET)

2 Corinthians 7:10-11 provides us with characteristics of genuine repentance.[65]

> *For godly grief produces a repentance that leads to salvation without regret, whereas worldly grief produces death. For see what earnestness this godly grief has produced in you, but also what eagerness to clear yourselves, what indignation, what fear, what longing, what zeal, what punishment! At every point you have proved yourselves innocent in the matter.* (ESV)

The counseling team should see evidence of these things in the lives of the counselees in increasing measure.

Earnestness-The counselee should demonstrate a willingness to submit to ecclesiastical discipline and the accountability of the counseling process (1 Cor. 10:12; 2 Cor. 7:8). We know the counselee is repenting when they voluntarily admit to their sinful behaviors and can see them

---

[65] We are grateful to Chris Moles for teaching us the specific application of these verses to domestic abuse counselees

as an abuse of power or control. They will begin to take responsibility for their thoughts and actions, seeing God as the standard for their responses. They will start to acknowledge sin without being prompted. He or she will admit and confess their own critical thoughts before they grow into bitterness.

He or she will be sincere in creating and executing a specific, concrete plan of action. This plan details what their "put off/put on" will look like, and they are determined to work it for the glory of God, not primarily to get their spouse back home (Eph. 4:22-24). We begin to see the fruit of heart change as the counselee expresses gratitude for their spouse's patient endurance (Ps. 51:6-12; Lk 19:1-10).

Eagerness- The repenting person will demonstrate an eagerness to make things right with all those harmed by their actions. Repenting counselees recognize that they have turned others against their spouse by sharing their "concerns" of their emotional state, parenting style, or response to being sinned against in abuse. They repent of resentment and gossip and frequently ask us if it is appropriate to go to those they gossiped to, to make things right. They do not hesitate to deal with their heart issues and then move forward by putting the necessary changes into action.

Indignation- They recognize their unjust treatment of another and are angry at their sin. There is an admission they have wrongly assumed the moral high ground over their spouse, and they humble themselves. The emotion of anger and indignation is turned towards solving the heart's problems, not attacking the person or people trying to help them change.

Alarm- As their sin's seriousness is realized, the abusive person becomes alarmed at the destruction, the pain, grief, and misery their sin has wrought. He or she begins to hate their sin (Ps. 32:5; 51:1-3) and experiences fear as they understand the impact of their sin on their relationship with God (Ps. 51:4; 2 Sam. 12:13) and others in their life.

Longing- Repentance is demonstrated by a longing for personal righteousness (2 Cor. 7:10-11). There develops an earnest desire to bring glory to God, and they stop consistently defending their own ideas and beliefs. Pride is replaced by an eagerness to confess what God calls sin and a reverent fear of God. There is a vehement desire to be free from their abusive thoughts, beliefs, desires, and actions. They long to put off critical speech, harsh attitudes, unloving communication, and self-worship, among other things and, they long to repent of the heart issues that drive them.

Such longings cause them to humble themselves and look deeply into God's Word for wisdom and insight. They ask God to reveal His thoughts to them. They revel in God's sovereign plan for their life.

Concern- There is now a concern for others instead of self-focus (2 Sam. 24:17; Phil 2: 3-4). The counselee begins to develop a deep desire to root out the evil in their heart and to gain victory over the specific sins identified as abuse in their life. This is displayed as compassion and concern for how their sin has affected his or her spouse. There is gratitude towards God for revealing their sin and enabling them to repent of resentment and bitterness. They deeply desire to honor God and love others more than they love themselves.

A repenting husband or wife will experience a sense of compassion and even joy at their recognition and change of heart toward their spouse and God. They recognize their spouse will sin toward them (Matt. 5: 11-12) and that they can exhibit the fruit of God's Spirit amid being sinned against (Gal. 5:22-23). The counselee agrees that the sovereign Lord put them together in marriage and that God expects they will exhibit the fruit of God's Spirit and not the fruit of unrighteousness.

Readiness to see justice done- A repenting person adopts a radical change in his or her worldview from self-serving rights and having to have their way to a Godly worldview that focuses on loving others more than they love themselves (Phil. 2: 3; Matt. 22:39). The counselee fully accepts responsibility for their actions (Ps. 51:3; 2 Sam. 24:10). They are willing to remain in the consequences of their sin for as long as necessary. They stop pleading and strategizing to get back together or move back to the home (if separated). The counselee becomes content to wait until the person(s) they harmed are ready to move forward. As the counselee embraces the truth that as a Christian, they are a bondservant to Christ, their beliefs will show an ongoing change in their thinking and behavior (1 Cor. 6:19; 1 Pet. 1:18-19). Instead of demanding their way, they will be at peace, trusting God to work out the details of their relationship as they obey Him.

Repentance is not something a person can conjure up from within. No amount of screaming or threatening, or other forms of manipulation can force a person to repent. Repentance is a gift from God (Acts 11:18; 2 Tim. 2:25). The abusive spouse must repent and demonstrate change for a significant period of time before being confident genuine repentance has occurred (Matt. 3:8; Ps. 51:4). How long this takes varies and is influenced by the level of abuse, length of time abuse has been taking place and the counseling team's consensus regarding their repentance. Our experience with domestic abusers has taught us that they can feign repentance (behavioral change) for a long time, usually long enough to get back in the home, before they revert to their previous behaviors (Rom. 16:18). Wisdom and discernment are needed (Prov. 15:22).

The victim must also confess and repent of the sinful heart attitudes and actions that have developed due to suffering such treatment. Often the victim perceives themselves as the righteous, wounded party. They adopt a self-righteous position and appear to believe that their spouse is not as spiritual or as acceptable to God as they are. They communicate through verbal and non-verbal means that their sin is not as egregious and almost literally peer down their nose at their spouse, "The Sinner." In these situations, the spouse must be confronted about their sinful attitudes toward their husband. They must be called to account on these numerous levels.

Often, the victim-spouse will come to counseling with the expectation that their oppressor will be the only one challenged, rebuked, or corrected. They see their oppressor as the only one who needs any kind of change! They are often very offended when confronted about their sin, saying things like, "This is not why we are here." "Why are you picking on me?" "What about him/her?" This leaves little room for self-examination and little room for accepting any responsibility for their sin. There is often an admission such as, "I am not perfect either," but there is much more focus on pointing out their spouse's wrongs. They both must learn and practice biblical ways of interacting with each other.

Rich presented as a man unwilling to admit he had been unloving, domineering, abusive in his speech, and even physically abusive to his wife. He was also reluctant to admit to being a serial adulterer. Initially, he was defensive and minimized, justified, and excused his sinful treatment of her. Rich didn't see the seriousness of his behavior before God or his wife. Though he professed to be a Christian, it became clear he did not have a right understanding of God, His righteousness, or an understanding of his sins, including his wife's abuse.

With the introduction of Scripture (2 Cor 7:10-11; Gal 5:19-21, 22-24; Col 3:5-16), Rich was shocked and alarmed at his standing before God and understood his need for a regenerative relationship with God. He began reading and seeking counsel and realizing the false teaching of his previous church; he began attending a church that taught solid bible doctrine and was saved.

Once converted, Rich immediately ended his adulterous relationships, confessed to his wife, counselor, and family members his abuse of his wife and his sins before God. He was now eager to establish relationships within the church and sought meetings with mature men in the faith.

His counseling sessions centered on his relationship with God and not on behavioral steps needed to reunite with his wife. He came to hate his sins and the effects they had on his wife and family. He was concerned for their welfare above his own. As those in his life processed his confessions, he accepted his behaviors had created anger and trust issues in his wife and extended family. He embraced his homework assignments and shared what he was learning and practicing with his wife and others.

After a time, his wife noted the changes in her husband's demeanor, change in heart motives, and external behaviors asked to return home. His behavior and devotion to God and his wife continued, and his wife readily noted the ongoing changes in her husband.

Through the counseling process, we also find that even when the abusive spouse has dealt with their sins biblically, there is much work yet to be done by both the abusive spouse and their victim.

There is a mistaken belief or understanding that repentance is "one and done" when the abuser repents, according to 2 Cor. 10:7-11, he or she is "fixed." This misbelief that the spouse will never return to any sinful behaviors of the past fosters the idea that every "failure" means they are not repentant. This is not and cannot be accurate. It must be understood that no Christian is ever free of all sin in this life. Perfection or a complete absence of sinful behaviors is not possible. Of course, physical assault and sexual abuse are never acceptable and should not be tolerated. We don't accept a person punching walls, slamming doors, or scaring their spouse and kids daily, and we do not send a woman back to someone who will continue to abuse her as before. We understand that the victim of abuse is afraid, even after their spouse has repented. Many of the people we help have been grievously sinned against and, they are self-protective. They simply do not want to be hurt again!

Garrett and Dominique have been married for five years and have three young children. They came for counseling due to Garrett's destructive patterns of name-calling, blaming, and extremely critical attitudes and speech toward Dominique. Dominique reacted to this ungodly treatment by lashing out in anger and deep-seated bitterness. In response, Garrett escalated his attempts at intimidation and control by grabbing her, pulling her, and shoving her around.

Recognizing they were in deep trouble, Dominique confronted Garrett, and he responded by making further threats. She took the kids and went to stay with her parents for a week. During this week, Dominique issued an ultimatum; either we get counseling, or she would leave him for good. This couple came in desperate for help, and Dominique was fearful that divorce might be her only option.

In the initial separate meetings with Dominique and Garrett, they completed safety and abuse assessments. It was essential to determine if it was safe for Dominique and the kids to be home during counseling. The pastor was contacted, and a counseling team was formed. Due to Garrett's escalating behavior that included pushing, shoving, and blocking her from seeking safety, the counseling team concluded a period of separation would be needed. Garrett moved in with his parents, and Dominique and the kids returned home.

Initially, Garrett was angry and unreceptive to biblical counsel. He was indignant and continued to bring up concerns about his wife's behavior. The counselor challenged Garrett on being defensive, refusing to accept responsibility for his own thoughts, beliefs, and actions. After several weeks of counseling, meeting with his mentor, and participating in the counseling process, Garrett began to take responsibility for his own behavior. In time, Garrett began to see changes in his heart attitudes and was eager to face his own sinful thoughts, beliefs, attitudes and to change his behavior. He became concerned for his wife and was ready to alter both his heart toward God and his resulting behaviors toward Dominique. His hatred of sin was evident, and he recognized the need for accountability. He experienced concern for the effect that his actions had on his wife and children.

Together with his counselor, Garrett created a plan for change. He began reading and memorizing Scripture. He identified the idols of his heart that led him to idolize Dominique. He and the counselor addressed his heart of anger, desire for power, and control that flowed from his self-worship. Garrett grieved over how his sin had affected his wife and desired to make it right with her. He realized that being out of the home until Dominique was comfortable with the changes she saw in him was much more important than Garrett's desire to be home with his family.

Over time, Garrett's pastor, friends, and even his golfing buddies noticed the changes taking place in Garrett. Confident that repentance was evident, the counseling team proposed to Dominique that she consider a group meeting with Garrett and the counseling team. This couple continued individual and eventually couples counseling until Dominique was confident Garrett's repentance was genuine, and the reunification process could safely begin.

When someone has been deeply hurt, it is natural for them to be suspicious of those who hurt them. They become hyper-vigilant and become very wary of the actions and motives of their spouse. The victim perceives that the abusive spouse is always plotting and scheming some new hurt. In some cases, we have seen the victim be irrational about their repentant spouse's actions and seek to demonize them in every respect. The victim is never satisfied with the repentance, change, or progress the offender makes.

It should be noted that people who are not abusive can say cruel things, be self-centered, and idolatrous. Going forward, will there be arguments? Yes. Will he or she get angry? Yes. Sometimes even yell and holler? Yes. Both people are still *sinners*. They would do well to remember they still have sinful natures and that they both will continue to struggle with their flesh (Rom.7:15-25).

In the repenting person, we will see self-correction when they realize they are headed down a previous path of oppressive, coercive, and controlling behaviors. They will examine their heart and address the sinful thoughts, beliefs, and desires that provoked those behaviors. The spouse who has repented of abuse will not continue to intimidate, coerce, demean, degrade habitually, and verbally assault their spouse. As they are working on their sin issues and are making progress, their spouse must be willing to allow them to show it. At some point, they must be allowed to earn trust. We cover this in-depth in the section on Reconciliation.

Philippe was separated from his wife, Carol, due to his emotional and verbal abuse. There was also an isolated event of pushing her onto the bed. Philippe has begun to demonstrate the fruits of repentance in his interactions with his counselor and church mentor. He has repented, and there is evidence of actual heart change. Philippe has done so well in counseling that the team and Carol decided it was time for them to begin to interact with each other. Philippe has confessed his sin to Carol and has asked her forgiveness. Carol has been down Apology Lane before with Philippe; more times than she can remember. She is not sure this is for real and has even told the counselor that she doesn't know why this time will be any different. Carol does not trust Philip's words or his new actions and is always looking to catch Philip in some act of deception. She is critical of his profession of change, and it shows in everything she says and does concerning Philippe.

Carol told her counselor that she was scared that Philippe had not changed at all. She pointed out several things "the old Philippe," said in recent conversations. She said, "This is not working. I don't think he is repentant at all!" Any changes Philippe has made, supported by good reports from the accountability he has in place and successful navigation of all the hoops Carol has him jump through, is never good enough. She is always looking for that one shred of evidence to prove to herself, the counselor, their friends, but most especially to Philippe that he hasn't changed one little bit. She thought he needed to be confronted and asked if this was not evidence of his old controlling behaviors

----

Specific Counseling Issues

Heart Issues

As previously stated, we focus on the heart as the motivator for the thoughts, beliefs, and desires that drive our actions and the words we speak. We believe that all domestic abuse and oppression proceed from the heart. Therefore, for the counsel to be effective, the heart must be the target of the counseling. Focusing only on the behaviors will, in the long run, be ineffective.

Every counselee is different, and the experienced counselor will have sufficient knowledge and understanding to recognize the fruit issues of the victim's heart that will arise in the counseling process. Therefore, we will only cover those that can be very problematic when helping victims work through their own heart issues. These sin issues may or may not exist because of the abuse, but they are problems that could complicate the reconciliation and reunification phases down the road. We have also included some of the homework and resources we use in these situations.

There is no repentance

I (Julie) am routinely involved in cases in which the husband does not repent. In some cases, years of biblical counseling and discipleship have done little to affect even lasting behavior change. This *should* trigger Matthew 18 in the church. However, in far too many situations, it does not. It may be that the church the couple belongs to does not practice restorative discipline. One or both people are not church members, so the church has no standing to discipline the unrepentant spouse. The other sad possibility is the church is unwilling to take any action to assist the spouse who is seeking their help and "sides" with the person committing the abuse out of a mistaken belief that he or she is repentant. It is easy to say, "Well, just leave and find a different church," but the church is often the only place the victim has for support. Leaving your church is (and should) be the last resort as it is a big decision.

When the abusive person does not repent, it is discouraging, sorrowful, and even provokes hopelessness in the victim who wants their marriage and loves their spouse. Many of these situations go on for years both before and after the intervention. Our counselees often express exhaustion and a desire for it to be over. Remind him or her that God continues to specialize in the impossible. There is always hope, as long as there is breath.

Suggest the counselee read, meditate, and respond to the Scriptures such as Psalms 4, 62, 68, and 73. You can make the Psalms homework assignments or work through them together with him or her in a counseling meeting. The goal is to help them see their situation through God's viewpoint.

Sufferology

Ultimately, the counselee will learn to suffer biblically. Sufferology is not a popular doctrine among Christians, but it will be necessary for them to know how to suffer well. 1 and 2 Peter contain valuable counsel for a person in a season of suffering. We suggest our counselee immerse themselves in these two epistles to gain wisdom and direction for how to suffer. For example, the counselee can "arm" themselves by adopting Christ's attitude (1 Pet. 4:1). Put their suffering in perspective with eternity in view and pray (1 Pet. 4:7). Learn to rejoice in what God is doing in them as they suffer (1 Pet. 4:12-13) and seek to glorify God as they are doing so (1 Pet. 4:16).

Dr. Robert Kellemen has done excellent work on sufferology, and we often use his book, _God's Healing for Life's Losses,_ with our counselees to help them with this during the counseling process.[66] In this book, Dr. Kellemen "climbs in the casket" of grief with the reader and takes them through the process of grief and suffering. The Psalms are also very helpful for developing a theology of suffering.

Identity in Christ

Anyone who has lived in a relationship where they are routinely subjected to contemptuous, coarse, insulting, hurtful, demeaning, and destructive words may not

---

[66] While not a workbook in the classic sense, this working-through book contains enormously helpful insights. Its focus is on the Scriptures to aid the sufferer to move forward

understand that she is of equal value before God.[67] Many abuse victims are dealing with the same problem- suffering abuse has become or significantly shaped their identity. Their anthropology of self (their identity) has been framed and determined by their phenomenology- their experiences, their thoughts, and beliefs about who they are now, in light of being abused.

A husband who abuses has conditioned his wife (intentionally or not) to think of herself as someone who doesn't measure up, who falls short, is incapable, incompetent, or a failure. When the wife abuses, the husband's identity as a protector, provider, and leader is usurped. He looks at himself as incompetent, a failure, and in need of his wife's correction. It is true, experiencing abuse can devastate a person's spiritual identity leaving them feeling betrayed, empty, and hopeless.

Many abused people do not understand their *Imago Dei*- -their creation in the image of God (Gen. 1:26- 28; Ps. 8:4- 5). Their identity has been mired in their victimization; therefore, as much time as needed should be taken to help them develop a biblical view of their position and identity in Christ (Eph. 1). Identity and answers for the problems that plague the soul are found in Christ.

The Christian has an identity, and to embrace it, they must begin to learn what the Bible says is true about them. As a regenerated person, their ability to grasp what it means to be "in Christ" becomes the foundation and is critical to their ability to move forward (2 Cor. 5:17). Through the lens

---

[67] See Anne Dryburgh, *Debilitated and Diminished,* 49 – 66, and Justin Holcomb, & Lindsay Holcomb, *Is It My Fault?* 84 – 86, 94 – 105.

of Scripture, they will see what is true, and by God's grace, they will accept what is true about themselves according to the unchangeable standard of God's Word. Studying, memorizing, and meditating on the Word of God will break down the cycle of destructive thinking and the belief system that defines them by the past.

We might have the counselee access Bible verse lists by typing "Who Am I- Bible" into their computer browser. These lists are a shortcut to help them fight the battle of thinking negatively about themselves. Scripture can remedy the human soul and provides the standard of truth. The "Who Am I" Scriptures tell them who they are in Christ and encourage them to focus on the things that are true and real (Phil. 4:8). They will experience joy and hope in the Lord as His Spirit uses the Word to encourage them and to enable them to live their lives for Him. The Christian should have as their objective, not a 'good' or 'positive' self-image, but rather an accurate self-image based on biblically correct perceptions and evaluations.

David Powlison provides further insight into the trauma survivor. He says,

> What happened to you is not the last word on who you are and where your life is going. It's a significant part of your story, but it's not the *most significant* part of your story. It's only one part of the new story of your life that Jesus is writing.[68]

Pastor and biblical counselor Steve Viars says, "When we open the pages of God's Word, we find a rich theology—

---

[68] David Powlison, "Recovering from Child Abuse," (Greensboro: New Growth Press; 1st edition, 2008), 5.

a framework of truth—to help us think about the past."[69] The counselee can become more like Christ in the process of sanctification, living out their new identity in Christ. This is not merely a renovation of character, but a change in the Christian's entire lifestyle. These changes begin in the heart and overflow into life and are demonstrated by continued growth and change (Eph. 4:22-24). It is God's continuing work in the counselee's life so that they increase in desire and do his good pleasure (Phil. 2:12-13).

Help them understand that their identity in Christ is crucial to overcoming the problems and effects of the trauma they have endured in the abuse. They no longer must view themselves as victims of past traumas, which may shape them but do not define them.

When survivors accept their new identity in Christ, it will help them cast off the thoughts and beliefs that lead to feelings of discouragement, despair, doubt, and depression. Even amid pain, hurt, and residual feelings of guilt and shame, those who embrace their new identity in Christ can experience God's provision of comfort, healing, and hope.

For homework, we often recommend the counselee read books like *The Attributes of God*, by A.W. Pink, or *Because He Loves Me,* by Elyse Fitzpatrick. We will also assign Matthew or John's gospel and have them write out how God sees them. For women, I (Julie) have my counselee write out how Jesus related to women in those two Gospels.

---

[69] Stephen Viars, "Redeeming Your Painful past: Present Grace, Future Hope" (Greensboro: New Growth Press, 2012), 5.

Identity as a Victim

In our work with those affected by abuse, we see two different responses to that treatment: the first is the person embraces the victim's identity. The other is the person accepts they have been victimized without identifying themselves as a victim.

The very nature of abusive behavior is the wielding of ungodly coercive power and control over another person to establish themselves as the dominant one in the relationship. As demonstrated previously, numerous tactics and behaviors are employed to diminish and subjugate their spouse and keep them under the abuser's control. We cannot state this strongly enough. We want to be very clear: counselee's in oppressive and abusive marriages *are* victimized by their spouses, but they don't have to make it their identity.

One notable biblical example of victimization is Joseph. Joseph was the beloved son of Jacob and Rachel, and his brothers abused him. In Genesis 37, we read that Joseph's brothers were jealous, envious, and hated him. There were ongoing conflict and hostility towards Joseph (vs. 2-4, 5,11). They plotted to kill him (v 20) but settled for throwing him in a dry well (v 24) and then sold him as a slave (v 28; Gen. 42:21). His victimization didn't end there. Eventually, Joseph became a slave to Potiphar the Egyptian (v36.) He was falsely accused of attempted rape and thrown in jail for two years (Gen. 39:20; 41:1) and forgotten by someone he helped to free from prison (Gen 40:23) before he was released and placed in a position of authority (Gen. 41:41, 46).

John MacArthur states regarding Joseph, "Years of suffering, pagan presence, and separation from his own family had not harmed his faith."[70] Even though Joseph was a victim of abusive treatment, he never lost sight of God's sovereignty in his situation, and he did not take on the identity of a victim. He recognized God was at work in and through him, despite his being falsely accused and imprisoned. He knew that God used his brothers' evil actions to bring about good (Gen. 45:8). Genesis 50:20 reveals his understanding. He said, *"As for you, you meant evil against me, but God meant it for good in order to bring about this result, to preserve many people alive."*

Rome and the Jewish religious leaders victimized the Apostle Paul. Time and again, Paul was persecuted by those who opposed the message of the gospel preached to both Jews and Gentiles (Acts 13:50; 14:1-6;19; 16:16-24; 17:5-9; 18:12-13;19:21-41; 21:27-36; 23-25; 2 Cor. 11:24, 26).

Neither of these men took on the identity of "victim." Neither man deserved the abusive treatment they received. We think it would have been easy and even understandable for either man to focus on being treated so horribly and how unjust their circumstances were. Were they victims? Yes, but they chose not to take on that identity. Instead, they converted their oppressors, brought others to faith, and displayed forgiveness and grace toward those who harmed them; they saw what happened to them as under the sovereign, wise hand of God. They both grew in their faith and changed as a result of what they endured. Joseph and

---

[70] John MacArthur. "The MacArthur Bible Commentary" (Nashville: Thomas Nelson, 2005), 69.

Paul saw their suffering had a purpose, and they determined to honor and glorify God in the midst of it.

However, in sharp contrast, what we have seen is that some of our counselees adopt a victim identity. The fruit of this misplaced identity is visible in their words and actions as this mindset is perpetuated. They display bitterness, rage, criticalness, judgmental attitudes, anger, hostility, pride, and self-righteousness (1 Sam. 13:11-12).

Our counsel must relate to the pain of the abuse they have endured and address the emotional torment brought on by keeping records of wrongs and unforgiveness. Also, assist the counselee in recognizing God's purposes in their suffering and embracing their identity in Christ, not in what they have experienced (Jn. 10:10).

Grief and Sorrow

The spouse who has been abused will be understandably sorrowful and will likely experience many layers of grief. Grieving is necessary and appropriate. Being sinned against by your spouse is exceedingly painful. Waiting for your unrepentant spouse to repent is painful as well. You should expect to see the intensity of grief wax and wane over the course of counseling.

The spouse who has been oppressed will grieve the lost years of their life and marriage, the hopes and dreams of what they thought marriage would be. We cannot say strongly enough that they must be allowed to grieve. You can expect to see grieving begin if the couple is separated for a few weeks or longer. We have had people describe it as coming out of a fog. Suddenly things are clearer than they have been in a very long time, and the realization of their situation brings deep sorrow and grief.

We find our counselees have benefitted both in session and as homework from Kellemen's *God's Healing for Life's Losses* as well as an excellent article, *I'll Never Get Over It- Help for the Aggrieved,* written by David Powlison. It is helpful for the counselee to work through how they are grieving over being hurt. The article is raw and real. In an abusive marriage, one spouse has been affected by the sin of the other. The person they entrusted themselves to has harmed them in ways they never thought possible. Powlison says,

> You won't forget. But you do not need to endlessly revisit what happened. You do not need to be imprisoned in the complexities and dead ends of your instinctive reactions...We are complex creatures wired to respond to wrongs in complex ways...Our reaction to grievous wrongs are muddy, not tidy.[71]

There is a balance between immersing oneself in feelings of grief and loss and working through them as part of sanctification. As the counselee deals with their grief, we point them to Jesus, the healer of their deepest wounds and their beautiful Comforter. We want them to see that He is entirely sufficient to be their joy, even amid sorrow. He loves them unceasingly, comforting them, accepting them, and will never leave or forsake them (Heb. 13:5). Help them

---

[71] David Powlison, *I'll Never Get Over It- Help for the Aggrieved,* in: *The Journal of Biblical Counseling, 28:1,* (Christian Counseling & Educational Foundation, Glenside, PA. 19038) 8-27

identify ways to discipline their minds to focus on Jesus in their grief (Ps. 42:6).

We also direct our counselees to the Psalms of Lament for comfort.

Psalm 3-7; 12; 13; 22; 25-28; 35; 38-40; 42-44; 51; 54; 55-57; 59-61; 63; 64; 69-71; 74; 79; 80; 83; 85; 86; 88; 90; 102; 109; 120; 123; 130; 140-143

Some people really love to write, and for them, assigning a Thought Journal as homework is very beneficial. We suggest they set aside a time each day to write their thoughts down on paper. We discuss them as part of the session and seek the Scriptures for wisdom concerning their thoughts and grief response.

Pride

As previously stated, pride is the primary root in the heart of a person who abuses another. Pride can also contribute to a refusal to forgive or reconcile a marriage after repentance is evident. A prideful heart is, in part, what hinders people from repenting of their sins. Like carbon monoxide, the sin of pride is often invisible to the person struggling with it. Also, like carbon monoxide, pride is deadly (Prov. 6:16-17a, 15:25-26; 16:18)

Pride kills the person's ability to see their own sin in a situation, so they justify their past behaviors, blame their spouse, and are critical of them. Pride elevates self above others, so demeaning words and attitudes are typical (Ps. 59:12). Pride is toxic and blinds the person to their heart issues, even when faced with the truth. Pride feeds their Pharisaical thinking and results in further divisions between them and their spouse. We address these behaviors and thought patterns as they are almost always present, especially in the initial sessions. Telling someone these things are true about them is not helpful. Like the person who has been breathing carbon monoxide, the prideful counselee is confused and unable to think straight. They are in a sin-filled fog of self-righteousness (Prov. 20:9; 30:12). We have to expose them to fresh air to clear the poison from their system to think and process clearly. We do this by asking questions that reveal their heart to them. For example:

- How is what you are saying, not self-pity?
- How is what you desire not self-indulgent?
- In this scenario, who is God?
- Are your thoughts and desires self-serving or others-focused?
- When you said ( ), who is being worshiped?
- When you said ( ), who is the idol of your heart?
- Are you submitting to God or self?

These questions and others like them can be used by the counselor to prick the counselee's conscience and expose the heart. The goal is to help them see that their thoughts, beliefs, and desires are focused on themselves as a god.

I (Bill) bring to light prideful heart motives in the early stages of counseling. I want him to see that his heart is focused on himself. Together we examine his heart motives, which typically are similar to these:

- I am right/you are wrong
- My wants are legitimate and godly
- My desires need to be fulfilled
- My spouse should ().
- I deserve respect/honor

His focus on himself and his sinful thoughts, beliefs, and desires lead him to develop:

- Critical spirit
- Anger/bitterness
- Alienation
- Fear
- Loneliness
- Judgmentalism

We also use Stuart Scott's booklet, *Pride and Humility,* both in the session and as homework to display how pride is present in their heart. This booklet contains 30 statements supporting Scriptures that describe manifestations of pride and will potentially cut through the fog and reach the counselee's heart.

Confronting pride is an ongoing issue in counseling, especially during the Recognition and Repentance phases. We hope the counselee will recognize their prideful heart motives and begin to address their heart's thoughts, beliefs, and desires. This is part of the reason for assigning homework. We desire to teach the counselee how to self-counsel, take what they learn in the session, complete the homework, and apply it throughout their daily lives. When the counselee comes to a session and begins to tell us how they overcame a prideful thought, belief, or desire by applying something they learned in counseling, we know they are making progress.

Idolatry

One area we would spend a generous amount of time examining is how domestic abuse is a revelation of heart-level idolatry, i.e., self-worship (Col. 3:5; 1 Cor. 10:14).

Idolatry is at the root of the power and control the abuser exerts over his or her spouse. It is a misbelief that allows them to justify using the tactics of oppression and abuse found on the Power and Control Wheel.

In Ezekiel 14:3, God, when talking to the elders of Israel, says, *"Son of man, these men have set up their idols in their hearts and have put right before their faces the stumbling block of their iniquity."* (ESV) An idol is a person or a thing that the idolater believes will be the source of their satisfaction and solution to their problems (Ex. 32:1-4). As such, that mistaken belief drives them to further sin by demanding from their partner what they were never created to be or provide.

God told Israel that the human heart could take good things like possessions, money, children, and yes, even a spouse, and turn them into the ultimate thing. In their deceived hearts (Jer. 17:9), the abusive spouse can make their husbands or wives the most important thing in their lives. The abusive person unwittingly places their spouse in the position of being an idol because they expect that he or she will meet their perceived needs or expectations. They look to their spouse to give them the desired hope, meaning, and fulfillment that only God can provide (Ex. 20:3). Their spouse is no longer a child of God made in His likeness, but a tool for them to use to satisfy their often-unending neediness.

When a husband abuses or oppresses, his wife's identity is in his expectations. She is there to meet his needs. Therefore, he uses whatever tactics are available to him to establish control over her lest he loses the security, value, and significance he craves and that she represents. The demonstration of ungodly power and control over another person is evidence of idolatry. While the Scriptures do instruct a husband to be the head of his wife and the wife to be submissive to her husband (Eph. 5:22-23), those verses' intent is loving, godly leadership, and willing submissive following. Scripture does not give a husband the right to be harsh, dictatorial, or to dominate his wife sinfully.

A wife who abuses her husband demonstrates power over him verbally, emotionally, and sometimes physically. She may outspeak him, outthink him, or overpower him with words and emotions. She may have an incredible recall of details that confounds him. Her disrespect may look like sarcasm, jokes, or outright criticism of her husband's looks and abilities.

Few people who abuse their spouse accept they have made their spouse an idol of his heart. They often proclaim God as being number one in their priorities and beliefs, but their actions and passionate demands tell a different story.

Starts to Affect my relationship
to other people

Desire ➡ Demand ➡ Need ➡ Expectation ➡ Disappointment
"I Wish"   "I Will"   "I Must!"   "You Should"   "You Didn't"

⬇

Punishment

"Because you didn't, now I won't..."
Or "Because you didn't, now I will..."

The above diagram illustrates what we have encountered when counseling abusive men and women. Taken from Paul

Tripp's book, *Instruments in the Redeemers Hands*, the idolatrous heart's progression becomes clear.[72] There is nothing wrong with having desires; we all have them. Our desires begin in the heart, and many of them are good and God-honoring.

It is good to desire a godly wife or husband (Prov. 18:22, 5:19; 1 Pet. 1:16; Gal. 5:24; Mk. 10:45; Eph. 5:25; 1 Jn. 1:9). However, when desires become demands, sin is at the door. A demand says, "I will have this." This heart's attitude feeds the misbelief that the person is entitled to something, and they do not expect to be denied what they desire. Entitlement feeds the mistaken notion of "need." The abusive person wants their spouse to be their "everything." In this case, needs are ungodly expectations placed on their spouse. When those expectations are not met is when we see the tactics of abuse emerge. Disappointment in unmet expectations promotes a victim mindset that fuels the use of power, control, and anger. The oppressor's goal is to forcibly manipulate their spouse into compliance to give them what only God can provide. Therefore, it is idolatry.

Because the lusts of the flesh are never satisfied (Prov. 27:20), the demands for love, compliance, and worship will increase as the abusive spouse perceives their husband or wife's failure to serve them in the way they believe they are entitled to be worshiped.

---

[72] (Understanding Idols Diagram and text from Christian Family Chapel Resources https://cfcjax.com/mt-content/uploads/2017/06/understanding-idols-diagram.pdf accessed 9-21-2020 Based on Instruments in the Redeemers Hands pages 85-88 P&R publishing, Glenside, 2002)

It is very challenging to help a counselee see his or her heart of idolatry. Often, the abusive counselee is self-deceived and does not understand his or her actions are flowing from a heart filled with idolatry. We want them to see the importance of addressing these problems at the heart level. In the session or as homework, we will ask the abusive counselee to tell us their thoughts, beliefs, and desires; we want to hear them tell us what they think the real problem is. Often, he or she will say to us:

- My spouse should show me more love
- I should be respected/obeyed
- I am not understood
- My love for him/her is rejected
- I should be heard by him/her
- He/she is not meeting my needs
- He/she doesn't show me I am wanted
- I am ignored/unimportant
- My opinion/words/needs are discounted

Because the counselee is being denied the worship he or she desires, these actions and feelings result:

- Anger
- Blaming
- Keeps records of wrongs
- Self-pity
- Tactics of power and control
- Fear
- Loneliness

We show the counselee what God says about each of their thoughts, beliefs, and desires, and how they demonstrate a heart focused on self and self-worship. Using a series of questions like those below, we want to help the counselee examine the heart.

- Am I tempted to be controlling? If so, what need am I attempting to meet by the action I desire to take? (Phil. 4:9; Ps. 37:4; 34:9-10)
- Am I demonstrating power over my spouse? What is my goal in doing that? (Prov. 21:2)
- Am I looking to my spouse as a god? (Lev.19:4)
- Who is the source of my satisfaction/happiness? (1 Cor.10:7)
- Is my anger bringing about the righteousness of God? (Eph. 4:26; Jas. 1:20)
- Are my current desires self-focused or God-focused? (Phil. 2:3-4)
- Is my hope in God or my spouse? (Ps. 146:5)
- Is having what I want more important than honoring God? Whom am I worshipping right now? (Matt. 6:1; Prov. 16:2; Jas. 4:1-17)
- Am I a slave to the approval of my spouse and not a slave of God? (Gal. 1:10; 4:8)
- Does this thought/belief/desire glorify God? (Col. 3:5)

The victim experiences the idolatry dynamic differently; He or she quickly learns that as long as they continue to provide the desired response through obedience and compliance, their spouse may be nice, kind, loving, and accepting. There is peace in the home; life seems "normal," and they wonder if they only imagine that things are "bad." Many oppressed spouses tell us they feel crazy because these cycles come and go many times throughout the week (or the day). Their spouse is unpredictable, and they never know what will provoke disappointment and anger in them. The victim functions as the "need-meeter" for their spouse and becomes responsible for ensuring their spouse's happiness, contentment and that their emotional "love cup" is filled. Of course, this is impossible because the victim is being asked to meet the needs only God can provide.

Because people change in the concrete and not in the abstract, we have provided several suggested Scriptures and possible homework assignments related to their application.

Jonah 2:8- Can counselee provide 2 or 3 ways they have forsaken the hope and love of God in seeking approval and worship from their spouse?

1 John 5:21 & Psalm 16:4- One is an admonition, and the other explains the results of disobedience. What are five consequences you are experiencing in your life for having made your spouse an idol?

We also suggest having the counselee do a study on the Pharisees. They wanted Jesus to comply with their expectations as to what a godly person was like.

The counselee's willingness to do the homework or respond to their own heart tells us if they will be responsive in counseling. When they continue to point to their spouse, we learn their hearts are hardened toward repenting at the heart level. They will make behavior changes, but not heart changes.

We help the abused spouse learn how to lovingly, firmly, and biblically address the idolatrous demands made upon them. Oppressed and abused individuals are conditioned by their spouse's control and anger to give them the worship they crave and often demand. That created a fear of man's response that they must now resist (1 Jn. 4:18).

As part of the counseling process, we have the abused spouse write out various relationship scenarios. We use those scenarios as role-plays to teach them how to respond in ways that will confront their spouse's idolatry. We practice the new responses because we want them to communicate in the Reconciliation and Reunification phases of the *Roadmap* what they learn by doing the role plays. The new responses must become second nature. He or she must know and become proficient at responding in a way that confronts the attempted abusive behaviors and directs their spouse to examine his or her heart motives and points them back to God.

It is essential to understand that the abusive spouse must demonstrate biblical repentance before these interactions occur. They will begin in the safety of the counseling team for the comfort of the abused spouse. It would be very unwise to suggest a person attempt this approach without repentance and change on the abuser's part.

Resources we use include:
Pride to Humility, by Stuart Scott
The Process of Biblical Heart Change, Chapter 7- Idolatry, by Julie Ganschow and Bruce Roeder
When People Are Big, and God is Small, by Ed Welch
Gospel Treason, by Brad Bigney
The Self-Centered Spouse, by Brad Hambrick

Control

Coercive control is another constellation of behaviors in an abusive or oppressive relationship. First, let us remind you that not all control is bad, and a person who places limits on another is not necessarily coercively controlling them. We all have controls or limits on many things in our lives, and most of them are for our health and safety.

The recipient may have initially considered controlling behaviors such as calling when he or she got home, checking in several times each day, or immediately reply to an email or text to mean that someone cared about them and watched over them as indications of love and concern. However, over time these requests have become demands and requirements and are now oppressive and suffocating. Their spouse limits contact to only those people, places, and things of which he or she approves.

While many wives experience such controlling measures, husbands are also subjected to coercive control. Their wives will forbid them from hanging out with a guy they don't think is suitable company or is a bad influence. If he decides to maintain the friendship, she may attempt to sabotage the relationship by making it so difficult for the other guy that he quits the friendship. Some wives' tantrum if their husband wants to go hunting or on a fishing trip, withhold intimacy or refuse to talk or interact with him and make his life so miserable that he abandons his plans. If he must take time to care for an elderly or infirm parent, she might sulk and cry or become enraged that he is "putting your mother/father ahead of me!" Her needs (which are often emotional) must take precedence over anything else.

When one partner uses threats, coercion, or other means to force the other to "do things my way," or when they take away choices and dictate how something is to be done, it can be abusive control. When the controlling person receives pushback on their demands, they may attack, diminish, or demean their spouse. As previously stated, coercive control is a central component of abuse. In the book of first Corinthians, our Lord says that love does not insist on its own way (1 Cor. 13:4-5). This sinful desire is rooted in the heart of the abuser.

Part of our goal is to assist both individuals in this relationship to see that the desire and grasping for control demonstrate their sinful idolatry of self. We will use heart level questions to bring the abusers demands into the light and challenge the thoughts, beliefs, and desires that fuel them. These questions focus on a reward for the behavior, revealing a heart that wants to control events for their own self-will. Some of those questions are:

- What did you want to happen when you threatened ()?
- What were your thoughts focused on before you did ()?
- Is your love for him/her conditional?
- Were you motivated by selfishness?
- Who were you thinking about when you ()?
- What right does the Bible say you have to do ()?

We will continue to use the Thought Journal as homework to help the counselees see what is in their hearts before opening their mouths or using control over their spouse (Lk. 6:45). Because this is another aspect of idolatry, the counseling process would be very similar.

Anger

Anger is another tool used to establish and maintain power and control over another person. Very often, the couple is functioning under a mental list of perceived rights in the relationship. Even biblical truths are turned into mandates and are demanded from their spouse. A few examples are:

- I should be respected.
- My sexual needs must be met on demand.
- I must be heard/listened to.
- My needs must be met.
- I have a right to be forgiven (even though my actions haven't changed).
- I can withhold forgiveness (because your actions haven't changed)
- I am the sole authority in the home (hyper-patriarchy).
- You must perform your duties to my satisfaction.

When these perceived rights are violated or are not met, some form of angry response results; for example, both the oppressor and the victim will express they have a right to be respected and a right to be treated fairly. They will often tell us (from their perspectives) that they are being denied these courtesies. The resulting anger looks different from the abuser and victim. The abuser will employ threats or manipulations to force their spouse to respect them, even if the compliance is out of fear. The victim will plead with their abusive husband or wife to respect them and to be fair. When their pleas are ignored, anger festers inside, and bitterness grows. Their anger may come out in passive-aggressive ways, but the victim is usually careful not to be too overtly angry and incur more wrath.

Spouses also claim the right to express their opinions and to be understood. In an oppressive marriage, often the oppressed spouse is not allowed to have their own opinion. To offer an opinion brings scoffing, mockery, or degradation from their husband or wife. The oppressive spouse doesn't care about anyone's opinion or thoughts but their own. This fosters anger in the oppressed or abused person, especially when they are put down in front of others.

We most often see the abusive person's heart on display when they are denied their way. Getting their way is something they consider to be a right, and it is unthinkable to them that they would be rejected. Explosive anger and rage are the expected results when denied, and the victim will often go to extravagant lengths to meet their demands or expectations.

Abusive and oppressive people have a high demand for "love" and acceptance from the person they harm. They believe they are worthy of love and will go to ridiculous lengths to manipulate their spouse into loving them as much as they feel they should be loved. When their demands are not met, they become angry and punish their husbands or wives with silence, threats of personal harm (including suicide), and sometimes leave home for hours or even days to teach their spouse a lesson (Eph 5:33; 1 Pet.3: 1-7).

Our abused and oppressed counselees often have no idea how angry they are until they have some time and distance between them and their spouse. Abused people usually stuff down the emotion and anger inside, and sometimes the anger has been festering for years. In some cases, the rage has been internalized for a long time because expressing it rained down more abuse on them. In other situations, they are so occupied with avoiding danger and further abusive treatment that there has been little opportunity to contemplate how upset they are. So, once they are safe, some victims experience a surge of incredible rage and anger.

If separation was necessary, new reasons for anger could crop up. A husband or wife may be angry that their spouse has betrayed the trust they placed in them. If a husband has been removed from the home, all the responsibility for caring for the house and children falls on the wife. While they are grateful for the break from the oppression and abusive behaviors, a few of our female counselee's have expressed anger at the hardships this time of single parenting places on them. They are angry at how the abuse has affected their lives and those of their children.

God has given humans the emotion of anger, and the Bible does not prohibit becoming angry at sin. Not all anger is sinful. The Lord Jesus Christ experienced and demonstrated anger, but in no way did He ever sin in His wrath (Matt. 21:12-13, Mk. 3:5). God hates the violence of domestic abuse (Ps.11-4-5; Mal. 2:13-17, Prov. 3:31-33)!
The victim needs to learn the distinction between righteous anger and sinful anger and how to respond in a way that glorifies God. Consider the biblical commands we are given regarding what we are to do with the God-given emotion of anger (Col. 3:8). We would spend a significant amount of time addressing any issues of sinful anger (Prov. 14:16-17; 29:22, Col. 3:8, Jas. 1:20), bitterness (Heb. 12:15; Ps. 139:23-24, Eph. 4:31-32), and unforgiveness (Col. 3:12-13,

Matt. 18:21-22). They must see that their anger flows from the heart.

Regardless of the reason for anger, if it is not dealt with biblically, the person will become bitter, with its own destructive roots and fruit. Through the counseling process, we help the counselees recognize their sinful anger and accept that they are responsible for it. While the sin of abuse is horrific, there is no "grading scale" for evil in God's eyes. God does not take any sin lightly. As difficult as it can be for some to accept, the victim is as in need of God's grace and mercy as the abuser is. We know numerous victim advocate organizations will be enraged at the biblical command for the victim to look at their sin.

We encourage the counselee to begin to renew their mind by studying what Scripture says regarding anger (Rom. 12:14-21). They must accept that there can be only one godly response to sinful anger: repentance that leads to heart change.

We have found a word study of Ephesians 4:17-32 to be particularly useful when counseling both abusive husbands and wives confronting their out of control anger.[73]

4:17-19: A description of your former life
4:20-24: A story of your new life in Christ
vs. 20-21: You've not learned Christ this way
vs. 21: The truth is Christ
vs. 22: Put off your former way of life
vs. 23: Be renewed in your mind

---

[73] Robert Somerville, *Dealing With Anger Completely*! Handout available at: bobs@vefc.net

vs. 24: Put on the new self, what you are in Christ

vs. 25: Put on truthful speech

vs. 26-27: Be angry but do not sin

vs. 28: Put on honesty

vs. 29-30: Use of your tongue

vs. 31-2: More on anger

When a person is driven to change their pattern of responding angrily, they will wrestle with their thoughts and subsequent emotions. They have learned a habit, and any habit can be broken. It will take time and practice, but sinful thought patterns and angry responses can be overcome (Rom. 12:2). Using Scripture in Ephesians 4 for study and repentance and the Thought Journal has helped abusive people get additional control over the thinking that has nurtured their angry hearts and ungodly angry responses.

Bitterness

When anger is not addressed biblically and allowed to fester, over time, it becomes bitterness. Bitterness is unresolved, unforgiven rage and resentment. The emotion of bitterness is seething and constant. It is a bottomless cesspool of rotten feelings that burrows deep into the soul. Bitterness is a sin. Do not be deceived; a person cannot fool around with bitterness and expect it not to own them.

We are aware that some who work with abused women do not see bitterness as sin but as the justifiable result of something that has happened to the victim. They say the victims have been hurt, abused, and disrespected; therefore, they argue, the victim has the right to be bitter. Bitterness is justified by claiming that others are responsible for it:

"Under my circumstances, can you blame me?" The sinful actions and attitudes of resentment are masked by righteous indignation and therefore seem justifiable. The victim feels justified in her bitterness and does not want to acknowledge the effect on her spiritual life (Heb.12:15). We want to help her understand that bitterness's defiling nature affects those she comes into contact with.

As part of the counseling, they will work through *Perspectives and Understanding Anger Biblically*[74] and a packet entitled: *Overcoming Anger and Bitterness: The Heart of Forgiveness.*[75]

The counselee will have to process this information, so we don't rush them. This can take weeks or months of intensive biblical counseling in addition to working with a mentor. He or she must come to the place where they accept that, if their spouse is a believer, the sacrifice of Jesus Christ atones for their sin. God dealt with it at Calvary (Rom. 3:25, 1 Jn. 2:2; 4:10). We suggest you help the victim to see the level ground at the foot of the cross. As Christians, both husband and wife are righteous, forgiven, blood-bought, sanctified, and in Christ.

If their spouse is an unbeliever, remind the counselee that they are separated from God and apart from Christ. Do they want God to give their spouse the just punishment for his or her sins? Do they genuinely wish their husband or

---

[74] Debi Pryde & Robert Needham, *A Biblical Perspective of What to do When You Are Abused by Your Husband.* 50-52

[75] Julie Ganschow, *Overcoming Anger and Bitterness: The Heart of Forgiveness.* Available from: www.rgcconline.org

wife to be eternally condemned for abusing them? We encourage them to see their unsaved spouse through eyes of compassion and to pray for their salvation. As they pray for their spouse's soul, they fix their eyes on Jesus (Heb. 12:1-2). We suggest using Matthew 18:21-35 (The Parable of the Unforgiving Servant) for a person who struggles with an unwillingness to forgive.

As the counselee is striving to overcome old responses, they may confess they are wrestling with their thoughts and emotions because they have formed sinful habits. It will take some time to master new responses, but they will experience change quickly when they repent. We might assign the book *Good and Angry* by David Powlison as homework. There are questions within the chapters to help guide the reader toward repentance and change.

Biblical Confrontation: How to Confront Her Husband When His Behavior is Ungodly

I (Julie) have found Chapter 14 of *The Excellent Wife,* by Martha Peace, to be an excellent resource to teach a wife how to biblically respond to her husband when acting or speaking in an ungodly manner.[76] I will use Peace's *Eight Resources for the Wife's Protection* as the basis to instruct her in communicating biblically with her husband in conflict.[77] The wife needs to understand that her husband is still a sinner even though he will have repented from abuse.

---

[76] Peace, Martha, *The Excellent Wife*. (Focus Publishing, Bemidji, MN: 1998), 154.

[77] Ibid. 156.

I would teach her the principles of biblical communication (Eph. 4:24-32) [Appendix E]. Her husband will still struggle with sin, just as she does, and learning how to communicate biblically will help her honor God and give her husband wise responses in conflictual situations (Prov. 16:23). We would construct scenarios from past negative conversations with her husband, and she would practice biblical answers using the communication tools she learned in counseling. These tools are essential for the wife to have! Equipping her with biblical responses gives her confidence that it is permissible for her to answer him and emboldens her to do so. Having her write down the words she would use on index cards and review them helps her commit them to her memory.

I also want her to know how to respond when her husband sins against her (Rom. 12:21). I will have her recreate two or three common scenarios (word-for-word) that typically provoke confrontation or disagreement between them. Using role play, we will work through how she should respond to her husband in ways that are respectful and glorifying to God and do not feed his sinful behaviors. I will also teach her how to make a biblical appeal when they disagree on a course of action. I will again have her write down her responses (word for word) and practice them until she is comfortable. We will use those as opportunities for role-playing with me acting in the role of a difficult husband.

Another focus of counseling is how she can give her husband a biblical reproof (Luke 17:3; Eph. 4:15; Gal. 6:1;

Prv. 9:8).[78] This is one of those critical areas that she may be very fearful to undertake (1 Jn. 4:18). Wisdom requires the counselor to be cautious when suggesting a wife biblically rebuke her husband, especially if there is a history or threat of physical abuse. Some churches teach that a wife is not allowed to rebuke her husband. Biblical counselor Martha Peace says,

> A Christian wife does not have the option of whether or not to reprove her Christian husband who continues in sin. She is commanded to reprove him because her husband is also a Christian brother in the Lord.[79] (see Ezek. 3:7-21)

Peace also covers reproving an unbelieving husband.[80] Because the man is not a Christian, it is not wise to use Scripture in this case (Rom. 8:7). Peace suggests instead using biblical principles without quoting Scripture. It is very important to speak respectfully and honor the husband in delivering a reprove or rebuke. If her husband is unresponsive or mocks her, it is not wise to continue (Prov. 9:8). In this case, we will again role-play to learn how to engage with her husband respectfully and honor him while standing for righteousness. I will ask her to write down several word-for-word scenarios, and we will practice how she can respond to him so that she will be ready should a situation present itself.

---

[78] Ibid. 161.

[79] Ibid. 162.

[80] Ibid. 164.

The wife will also learn how to respond to unreasonable demands her husband might make (Prov. 26:4-5).[81] This would include what she can say should he make accusations or have ungodly, unrealistic expectations or demands. We will also cover seeking godly counsel from within the church for ongoing accountability and to assist in any new issues that would arise when the family is reunited (Prov. 24:6)[82]

Biblical Submission

Before discussing biblical submission in marriage, both the husband and the wife must understand what the Bible says about this critical doctrine. Because it is so often misunderstood and misapplied in the counseling process, we will cover this is in great detail.

We must begin with the creation, as it is foundational to understand God's created order and the roles of men and women as God designed them. Human beings are the crown of God's creation. Genesis 1 and 2 both document the origin of human life. Genesis 1:26 – 28 provides the account of the creation of mankind upon the earth. The Bible teaches that on the sixth day of creation, man was created from the dust of the ground (Gen. 2:7). The woman was created from the rib God took out of the man (Gen. 2:21 – 22). Gen. 1:27 informs the reader that Adam and Eve were created in God's image and likeness. To be made in the image and likeness of God means "man is like God and represents God."[83] Adam and Eve were of equal spiritual value to God and

---

[81] Ibid. 165-166.

[82] Ibid. 167-168.

[83] Wayne Grudem, "Systematic Theology: An Introduction to Biblical Doctrine," (Grand Rapids: Zondervan, 1994), 442.

were created to obey, serve, and love God. This makes human beings unique and distinct from anything else God created. It is significant in that while all creation may be beautiful, and much of it is intelligent, only humans share God's moral and spiritual qualities.

It is clear from Scripture and observation that there are differences between men and women. Apart from the physical and biological differences, the genders are intended by God to complete and complement each other. After God breathed life into the male, Adam, God declared he was incomplete without a suitable companion (Gen. 2:20). His Creator said it was not good for him to be alone (Gen. 2:18). John MacArthur says, "He was incomplete without someone to complement him in fulfilling the task of filling, multiplying, and taking dominion over the earth. This points to Adam's inadequacy, not Eve's insufficiency (cf. 1 Cor. 11:9). The woman was made by God to meet man's deficiency."[84] While God created Adam out of the earth's dust, God created Eve from Adam's rib or side (Gen. 2:21 – 23). "God used that rib in the creation of Eve. This account shows how important the woman is to a man: she is part of his very being, and without her man is incomplete. [sic.]"[85]

Eve brought to Adam what he lacked as his perfect complement. She was to be a helper suitable to his needs. With Eve, Adam could procreate and share in the details of life, both ordinary and intimate. Without Eve, he could not multiply and fill the earth, and he was simply lonely for someone like himself. Like Adam, Eve was expected to have

---

[84] John MacArthur. "The MacArthur Bible Commentary 14.

[85] James I. Packer, "Daily Life in Bible Times," Ed. James I Packer, Merrill C. Tenney, William White, Jr. (Nashville: Thomas Nelson Publishers, 1982), 21.

authority over God's creation. This authority did not belong only to the man. She was also commanded to be fruitful and multiply, replenish the earth and subdue it, and have dominion over every living thing in the sea, the air, and on the earth (Gen. 1:27 – 28). Adam's role and every husband's role is to be the leader, husband, and protector. He is to lead, care for, nurture, provide for, and sacrifice for his wife. Eve's role and the role of every wife is to follow, support, respect, respond to, and submit to her own husband.

In summary, the Bible teaches that men and women are different but equal. Women were created in the image of God and are equal to men in essence and value (Gal. 3:28; 1Pet.3:7). However, God created them with distinct differences and gave Adam and Eve unique roles (Eph. 5:23; 1 Tim. 2:12).

Both men and women are commanded to be submissive to authority. As Christians, we are first under God's ordained authority made known to us by his Holy Spirit, the writing in his Holy Bible, the church's authority (Matt. 18: 15-17; Heb. 13:17), and the authority of the government (Rom. 13: 1-5).

To submit means "to be subject to, or to rank under, or come under the protection of another."[86] Submission is a biblical doctrine that applies to every Christian regardless of their abilities, education, knowledge of Scripture, or spiritual maturity (Eph. 5:21). We are to submit to God and Christ because we are subjects of a Sovereign Ruler, and as such,

---

[86] *hypotasso* https://www.blueletterbible.org/lang/lexicon/lexicon.cfm?strongs=G5293

we are called to a life of humble obedience to His commands. Christians submit out of love and thanksgiving for what God in Christ has done for us (1 Pet. 3:18; 2 Cor. 5:17-19).

Submission and Headship in Marriage

A husband's headship and leadership in the home are taboo subjects and are misunderstood topics today. Culturally, headship is presented as having power over another person to dominate, minimize, and subjugate them. In some cases, the criticisms are valid as those with authority abuse it. Adding to the secular misunderstandings, the church does not always have clear teachings on male leadership, and abusive men warp God's instructions for their selfish purposes (Mk. 10:42-45).

As we have said, marriage is a partnership of two different but equal people, and both have unique responsibilities and different roles in marriage (1 Cor. 11:3: Eph. 5: 28-29). Understanding God-given design is imperative to challenging and teaching what needs to be repented of and what needs to be put on for the glory of God.

God has assigned headship in every family to the husband, not the wife (Eph. 5:23). Stuart Scott says,

> The husband must humble himself to realize that he does not have unlimited authority, (it is delegated authority), that his authority is not for his own benefit, and that his authority should be carried out lovingly.

> Both leadership and submission should flow out of a love relationship between husband and wife.[87]

Though their roles are different, both the husband and the wife function under Christ's headship, Christlike leadership gives husbands the obligation to serve their spouse sacrificially, rather than being served (Eph. 5:25-33; Matt. 20:27-28; Phil 2: 5-9; Jn. 13:16). Stuart Scott explains,

> He must put his wife before himself and serve her, even when it means a personal sacrifice on his part. Christ sacrificially loved us to the point of death. Our goal is to model our love after that of Christ. We must be willing to lay our lives down for our wife daily. A wife who is sacrificially loved will usually have no doubt of her husband's love (Eph. 5:25).[88]

There is a chain of submission presented in Ephesians 5:22-24:

> *Wives, be subject to your own husbands, as to the Lord. For the husband is the head of the wife, as Christ also is the head of the church, He Himself being the Savior of the body. But as the church is subject to Christ, so also the wives ought to be to their husbands in everything.*

This passage clarifies that God is the head of Christ; Christ is the head of the church, Christ is the head of every man, and man is the head of the woman (1 Cor. 11: 3). Just as Christ willfully submitted to His Father's headship (Jn. 6:38; 5:30; Matt: 26:39), husbands are called to submit to the Lordship of Christ. Likewise, women are also called to

---

[87] Stuart Scott, The Exemplary Husband, A Biblical Perspective, Revised Edition, Focus Publishing, Bemidji, MN, 77.

[88] Ibid. 82.

submit to Christ and then to their husbands leadership in everything (Col. 3:18; 1 Cor. 11: 3).

Unfortunately, marital submission is often perverted by an abusive husband to maintain power and control over his wife. Biblical Counselors Debi Pryde and Robert Needham remind us that no one has been given *absolute* authority over another person. Only God has that authority. A husband cannot righteously claim he has absolute authority over his wife. His leadership is legitimate only when it conforms to the Word of God. A husband cannot demand his wife submit to him; submission is freely given (Eph. 5:22).

The authors caution us to be "extremely careful" when advising an abused woman regarding submission. Often, if a woman is told to go "home and submit" to her abusive husband, abuse increases. "The husband takes it as a signal he can bully her and that it "proves" his abusive treatment is 'deserved.'"[89]

A woman who is being abused cannot righteously submit to abusive behavior. Refusing to accept being abused is *not* the same as being persecuted for righteousness sake (Matt 5:10) because it is *never* right to submit to unjustified evil without resistance. It is not disobedient or unsubmissive to expose abuse. Christians are called to overcome evil with good (Eph. 4:29-32; 5:14), and domestic abuse is undoubtedly evil.

Headship, leadership, and submission are areas we cover in-depth during the marriage counseling phase. Bill has the men read from Stuart Scott's book, *The Exemplary Husband.*

---

[89] Ibid. 45.

It becomes evident that the primary relationship is with God and not his wife. Abuse is not a relationship issue between him and his wife, but between himself and God. Julie has the women read *The Excellent Wife* or *Helper by Design*. Both these books present a biblical view of marriage and submission.

Additional Counseling Issues

Appendix F contains some additional heart issues that are frequently present in either the husband or the wife in abuse situations. The counselor will need to address these in the course of biblical counseling. There are excellent biblical counseling books, podcasts, blog posts, articles, and other resources available on these issues to assist the counselor and to assign to the counselee as homework.

Initial Homework

The counselee is expected to complete homework in the time between the sessions. Of course, a significant part of the homework is reading from the Bible. We want them to use their time focusing on prayer, Bible reading, and examining their hearts while completing the homework.

In addition to the books and resources we have already mentioned, we always assign either *The Process of Biblical Heart Change Workbook* or *The Process of Biblical Change* booklet.[90] We assign the workbook if the counselee needs instruction on Bible truths related to salvation, repentance from sins, and God's sovereignty, and the

---

[90] Both books available at Amazon.com

booklet for the counselee who is versed in these truths. Both resources emphasize the necessary changes of the heart the counselees must apply to effect Godly changes in their lives. The counselees are asked to devote 30 to 60 minutes to homework every day. The majority of heart work is completed between counseling sessions as the counselee prays, reads the Word, and makes application of the homework.

We expect that our counselee will complete and submit their homework before each session. We will spend time in the session discussing how the homework has affected their heart and how they have made application of what they have learned. If we do not receive the homework, we will initially give "grace" and meet with them one time. However, repeated failure at completing homework is an indication he or she is not as invested in the process of change as we would like. We will often cancel the appointment and ask them to return when they have completed our assigned homework.

Reconciliation

Navigating New Roads

Be Reconciled One to Another

We find reconciliation throughout the Bible as God sought to reconcile His people to Himself. God's people were treacherous, idolatrous, adulterous, selfish, wicked, corrupt, ungodly, foolish, and wayward, among other things (Isa. 1:1-31, Neh. 9:17, 1 Jn. 3:4, Gal. 5:19-21) and yet God in His infinite mercy condescended Himself and came in the likeness of man to be the perfect sacrifice for sin (Phil. 2:5-8). Christ made way for mankind to be reconciled to God, and He desires that we are reconciled to one another (Col. 3:12 – 13). Couples that have struggled with domestic abuse will navigate new roads individually and together in the process of reconciliation.

When to open the topic of reconciliation with the couple is a question we regularly receive. We stress that each situation is unique, and setting hard and fast timelines for reconciliation may not be wise. Instead, we suggest establishing benchmarks for the abusive spouse to meet.

One of the most important people to consult when considering reconciliation of the couple (when separation is in effect) is the person who was victimized. The decision for reconciliation counseling is not made until the counseling team is confident that the abuser is consistently demonstrating the fruit of repentance. The victim has worked through most of their heart issues, and they are ready for this step. We do not force them into reconciliation, as we must be very sensitive to the victim's fears and concerns. It is not wise to force the couple back together if one of them is not ready. The abused spouse is the one who will live with the consequences of reconciliation, and he or she must be confident their spouse will not return to reviling or physically harming them. We have had repenting spouses tell us they did not want to move home until they were confident of their ability to love their spouse unconditionally and their spouse's biblical repentance.

As the team (including the abused spouse), we look for repentance fruits to assess if the time is right to begin the reconciliation process. The bottom line is, when repentance is genuine, everyone will see it. Some things we look for are: 1) What is the repenting spouse's goal? Is it to "get back with my wife/husband" or glorify God by how they live their lives? 2) Is the repenting spouse able to recognize their sinful thoughts, beliefs, and desires and respond to the conviction of the Holy Spirit? 3) If they fall into sin, are they able to course correct? 4) Is the repenting person demonstrating spiritual growth and change (Eph. 4:22-24) How does the repenting spouse react/respond when they do not get their way?

We urge the team to allow the repenting abuser to demonstrate the fruits of repentance long enough that we can be reasonably confident he or she is not faking it. This is the risk of setting a timeline; the abusive spouse will effectively play "beat the clock" and often fake it long enough to get back in the home without having undergone genuine biblical heart change.

The Full Disclosure

As a part of the reconciliation plan, the repenting spouse is asked to write a full, detailed disclosure of their sin and offenses toward their victim (Appendix G). We consider the full disclosure to be as much, if not more, of a full disclosure of their iniquity before God as it is a disclosure of the sin they committed against their spouse (Ps. 51:4). The counseling team will interact with the repenting spouse and their statement over the next session or two to help assess the fruit of repentance and determine if they are ready for this next step or if more counseling is necessary.

When the repenting spouse writes the full disclosure, we are looking for them to take 100% responsibility for their behavior irrespective of their spouse's actions. They must start the sentences with the word "I" and not "you" and not in any way that is casting blame, fault-finding, blame-shifting, or accusatory. They must be specific as to what they did (their own behaviors), not what they intended to do ("I degraded you when I called you names," "I sinned against you when I wouldn't let you get medical care"). They must be specific about what they wanted (i.e., "I wanted you to shut up or leave me alone," or "I wanted you to listen to ME!").

We are looking for several key things: Does their sin grieve them? Do they understand the grievous nature of their sin before God? Do they see abuse the way God sees it? Is their confession more about them or the grief, sorrow, and pain that their sin has brought into the lives of their spouse and children? Are they making excuses for their actions? Alternatively, are they honestly owning their sinful behavior and demonstrating a changed heart? Does he or she ask for forgiveness for these actions? They must be truthful and expect nothing from their spouse. We make sure the repenting spouse understands that they are not to expect their husband or wife to say, "I forgive you," or "It's okay," or any other acknowledgment of their confession.

The Victim Impact Statement

When the victimized spouse is ready, we ask them to write out every word they would like to say to their husband or wife in a Victim Impact Statement (Appendix H). The statement can be as long or as short as they want it to be. However, we urge them to cover the months or years of abuse. The abusive husband or wife needs to hear how their actions have harmed and affected their spouse.

This process is often very painful and difficult for an abused woman. One suggestion I offer her is to suggest she write very simply, perhaps using a voice-to-text program that will allow her to focus on speaking instead of typing. The goal is to speak or write in a way that will help her husband identify with the abuse and trauma from her perspective.

Usually, we have the victim read the statement before the abusive spouse gives their full disclosure. The abused spouse has been profoundly impacted by the domestic oppression, emotional, verbal, spiritual, and physical abuse that has been done to them. They will be affected regardless of the length of time they were abused, and a part of the reconciliation process is for them to tell their abusive spouse how their words and behavior have harmed them.

Making this statement does not mean the victim can never again voice the past's pain or trauma. Depending on the abuse's length and severity, the victimized spouse may benefit from ongoing biblical counseling to put these issues to rest, even after the couple has been reunited.

Couple's Counseling

Providing that the Full Disclosure and the Victim Impact Statement session(s) go well, and the couple is ready, we make plans to initiate couple's counseling. Before the first couple's session, we ask both husband and wife to provide us with three to five issues they think need to be addressed in this next phase of the counseling process.

The issues raised should be formerly problematic or led to some form of abuse before counseling and intervention. We find the victimized spouse is understandably concerned and hesitant to bring up such issues because they previously led to abuse. The counseling team may need to provide a wife reassurance of safety and protection. Remind her that she is not dealing with the same man who abused her; he has changed and is demonstrating the fruits of repentance. Additionally, it is best for these issues to initially be brought to light in the counseling process where help and even intervention are available if needed. Discussion of difficult topics will demonstrate the growth, change, and repentance of both husband and wife.

We are initially very involved in the couple's sessions. We guide them as they discuss thorny issues with each other. We continue teaching, rebuking, correcting, and training the couple in righteousness as they talk (2 Tim. 3:16). We may stop them in mid-discussion to remind them of a biblical principle, ask them to rephrase or reframe something they said and use the biblical communication skills they have gained through individual counseling sessions. Suppose the conversation gets heated, and the repenting abuser begins to regress, causing the victimized spouse to become frightened or uncomfortable. In that case, the meeting is halted, one counselee and the counselor exit the room, and individual counseling resumes.

Throughout the couple's counseling, we gradually decrease our involvement in the couple's discussions until we are essentially observers of their interaction with each other. This evolves into marriage counseling and provides plenty of opportunities for the counselors to evaluate ongoing progress in repentance and change. The couple works through issues and problems that may have plagued the marriage apart from the abusive treatment. The number of couple's sessions is determined by need and progress.

If there are children in the family, we urge the couple to bring them for several sessions to answer any questions they may have and observe how they function with the kids in a controlled environment. There are plenty of opportunities for younger children to need correction in this setting, and it will often provide more fodder for the couples' counseling sessions.

Phone Conversations

As we continue to work toward reunification, we encourage the couple to talk together on the phone. Initially, the victim-spouse controls when the calls happen and how long the phone calls last. Creating a schedule can be a useful tool. As the comfort level grows and their spouse demonstrates the fruit of repentance, we encourage them to allow the phone calls to originate organically. The couple can predetermine topics of discussion, or they can continue conversations begun in the counseling session. The phone calls' length and content are initially up to the victimized spouse's comfort level.

Dating

We suggest the reconciliation process continue at a slow pace, whatever the victim-spouse is comfortable with. Once couples counseling and phone calls are underway and comfortable, we recommend the couple begin to spend time together. Initially, we advise they spend supervised time together in public. This could include meeting at church, attending the same small group, building up to meeting each other for a lunch or dinner date.

We suggest someone from the counseling team, or a couple from church who has been involved with the couple throughout this process, accompany our counselees on a double date. As this process continues, they can arrange to be at the same restaurant or venue discretely observing and providing a sense of safety for the victim.

Initially, the husband and wife should drive separately and arrive alone, providing a way of escape should something go awry for one of them. As the comfort level increases and the repenting abuser continues to demonstrate the fruit of repentance, they can go together to the place the date will take place. When the victim-spouse is ready, the other couple can drop out of the mix.

When the couple has demonstrated they can talk about difficult and problematic issues in our group sessions, marriage counseling is proceeding nicely. They are becoming comfortable with each other, and the team agrees that progress is being made. We prepare for the final phase: The reunification of the couple and family.

Reunification

Charting A New Course

Reunification is the final stop on the *Roadmap* and is necessary when the couple has been separated due to abuse. We are intentionally not emphasizing reunification because, with the exception of what is stated here, the couple continues to receive basic biblical counseling (i.e., conflict resolution, biblical communication, parenting, finances, etc.) At this point in the journey, the couple begins to chart a new course forward. They begin to spend more time together, and eventually, the family is reunited. After reunification, we recommend ongoing involvement with the church and counseling with the couple for the foreseeable future.

Easing into the Home

Once the counseling team and the victimized spouse are confident repentance and change will continue, the repenting spouse can begin to make visits to the home and interact in that setting with their spouse and children. Everyone must understand he or she is a *visitor,* not a resident. That is very important. While they are at the house, the visiting spouse should respect the boundaries the rest of the family or the counseling team has pre-established.

We suggest that home visits mimic what life will be like should the couple reunite. Consider including yard work with the family, watching movies, eating meals, and other "normal" activities. These opportunities give the repenting spouse a chance to parent their children, apply the counseling principles they have learned if difficulties arise, and continue to demonstrate repentance and change.

The repenting spouse-as-a-visitor phase might last a while. The victim-spouses we have worked with want to allow enough time to really learn if their husband or wife is trustworthy in "real life" situations. They are comforted by the knowledge that their spouse can be sent away if things get uncomfortable, especially at the beginning of these visits. When the victim spouse is ready, the repenting spouse can move back home.

It is essential that the couple remain engaged with the counseling team for the first several months after reunification. The frequency of counseling sessions will depend on the smoothness of the transition. It is at this point that the couple begins to merge back into life. We often continue to meet with the couple on a bi-weekly basis at this point, unless there are increased problems or conflict.

Our plan is to turn them over to the care of their church gradually. We suggest the church stay actively involved with the family for the first year after reunification. We remain available to the couple and the church for phone calls, consultations, and continued counseling if they choose or if we are needed.

Final Destination

You Have Arrived (Almost)

When on a road trip, some of the most welcome words to hear from the GPS are, "You have arrived at your destination. Your route guidance is finished." Unlike a road trip, our counselees have not truly arrived. They are not at the end of their journey because progressive sanctification is life long. However, the couple may be ready to merge back into church service and resume a more "normal" life.

We cannot express how important it is for the church to surround the reunified family and continue to walk with them in life. If possible, the disciples who have been ministering to the couple as part of the team should remain involved.

It is important not to be surprised when problems crop up in their relationship. Although repentant, the couple is not sinless. They may benefit from marriage counseling and individual discipleship to address new issues, but none of them should rise to the level of abuse. Over time, the need for intensive counseling and discipleship should decrease. The couple should reengage in the life of the church, attending small groups, Bible studies, and other activities that will provide accountability and replace the counseling team, which can now be disbanded.

The End of the Road

Working with abusive men and women continues to be a significant part of our ministry. We learn and grow with each situation that God gives us. We recognize that we have not addressed every possible issue or scenario in this edition and plan to refine and add to this material. We want to continue to assist pastors and biblical counselors to serve those affected by domestic abuse and violence.

If you are someone experiencing domestic abuse or oppression, we want you to know there is hope, there are people who do care, and you are not alone. If your previous attempt at getting help didn't go well, do not be discouraged; you face a very challenging life problem because domestic abuse situations are hurtful and complicated. Though it is challenging to ask for help and guidance, we want you to know that God is powerful, and we have seen Him change people's lives. Remember, God specializes in the impossible (Phil. 4:13; 2 Cor. 3:5; Rom. 4:21).

> Do not cling to events of the past or dwell on what happened long ago. Watch for the new thing I am going to do. It is happening already—you can see it now! I will make a road through the wilderness and give you streams of water there. Isaiah 43:18-19 (GNT)

Appendix A

The Abuse Risk Inventory (ARI)

Ask the counselee to circle the statements that describe how their spouse treats them.

1. Does your spouse's behavior, without warning, swing between loving, kind, and charming one day to cruel, explosive, and hateful the next?
2. Is your spouse critical of your efforts, particularly if you are happy or enthusiastic?
3. Does your spouse blame you for their failures?
4. Does your spouse angrily overreact if you cry or express emotional distress or dismay at their behavior?
5. Is your spouse extremely jealous of your friends and family?
6. Does your spouse wrongly accuse you of improper interest in the opposite sex?
7. Does your spouse expect you to account for every minute you are out of their sight, particularly when you leave home?
8. Does your spouse regularly or consistently disregard or discredit your views, feelings, interests, and preferences?
9. Does your spouse shove you around, bully you, or handle you roughly during a disagreement?
10. Does your spouse raise a hand or fist to you?
11. Does your spouse actually slap or hit you when angry?
12. Does your spouse grab your arm or neck roughly or painfully?

13. Does your spouse verbally attack or shout very loudly at you when angry?

14. Does your spouse become remorseful after an abusive incident, try to be kind after being very angry, and then begin to get cold and increasingly irritable as the tension builds until the next explosion?

15. Is your spouse frequently unreasonable or unapproachable during discussions?

16. Does your spouse threaten you with taking the children away or other "punishments" if you confide in someone else about what goes on at home?

17. Does your spouse appear to "punish" you with long periods of cold silence?

18. Does your spouse ever state or imply that he or she needs to "teach you a lesson?"

19. Is your spouse sarcastic and defensive with you when you try to discuss any of their problems with them?

20. Does your spouse belittle your accomplishments or your physical appearance?

21. Does your spouse curse at you or call you demeaning names such as "stupid," "fool," and so on?

22. Does your spouse react inappropriately or angrily, take personal offense, or claim to be "hurt" if you make a mistake?

23. Does your spouse attempt to isolate you from friends or family?

24. Does your spouse control the finances, so you have little or no discretionary funds?

25. Does your spouse resent the time you spend talking to friends or family members?

26. Does your spouse make rules for everyone else they don't have to follow?

27. Does your spouse become very angry if you break their subjective rules?
28. Does your spouse require you to get an approval of every purchase, no matter how small?
29. Does your spouse consistently criticize your spending habits?
30. Does your spouse change the subject or act defensively whenever you bring up a concern about them?
31. Has your spouse (recently or in the past) threatened self-harm or suicide?
32. Does your spouse appear confused and angry when you are not sexually responsive after unkind treatment of you?
33. Does your spouse rarely admit they are wrong or at fault?
34. Does your spouse resent the attention you give to the children?
35. Does your spouse tell the children when you have failed to do what you should, or in any other way encourage the children to disrespect you?
36. Does your spouse regularly undermine your authority in the home?
37. Does your spouse make rules and then change them without warning?
38. Does your husband insist that he would not be angry if you were more godly, submissive, or cooperative?
39. Does your spouse control your use of the phone?
40. Does your spouse not allow you to talk on the phone to your family?
41. Does your spouse limit, screen, or listen in on phone calls or read your emails?
42. Does your spouse block your way, prevent you from moving about, or prevent you from leaving?

43. Does your spouse deprive you of food or sleep?
44. Does your spouse use sex as manipulation or a weapon?
45. Does your spouse control or determine how you wear your hair, makeup, or choice of clothing?
46. Does your spouse prevent you from accessing medical care?
47. Does your spouse embarrass you, insult you, or put you down in front of others?
48. Does your spouse withhold affection as a way to punish you?
49. Does your spouse blame you for their behavior?
50. Does your spouse twist Scripture to support how they treat you?
51. Does your husband stress it is your duty to submit to his authority without question?

Appendix B

Make A Safety Plan

To increase safety during a violent incident, you may use a variety of strategies. Here are some strategies for you to consider.

I can use the following options:

1. What are the possible escape route(s) from my home? What doors, windows, elevators, stairwells, or fire escapes could I use? I will take the time to practice how to get out safely.

   _____
   _____

2. I can keep my purse/wallet and keys handy and always keep them in the same place (_____) so that I can locate them easily if I need to leave in a hurry. I can also have a second set of keys made if my partner/ex takes the first set.

3. I can keep a bag ready and put it_____
   _____ so I can leave
   quickly.

4. If it is safe for me, I could tell the following people about the violence and request that they call the police if they suspect I am in danger:_____
   _____and
   _____.

5. Children's safety in abuse situations is central to a safety plan. I may be able to teach my children a safety plan specifically for them in these circumstances. I can teach my children to use the telephone to call the police and the fire department.

6. It may be helpful to have a code word to use with my children, other family members, or friends if I could need them to call for help. I will use this word code:

    _____.

7. Safe places that I can go to if I need to leave my home. Be prepared even if you think you will never have to leave.
    *   A place to use the phone:_____

        _____

    *   A place I could stay for a couple of hours:

        _____

    *   A place that I could stay for a couple of days:

        _____

    *   I can teach these strategies to my children.

8. When an abusive incident occurs, I will move to a safer room. During an abusive incident, it is best to try to avoid places in the house where I may be trapped or where weapons are readily available such as the bathroom or kitchen. Bigger rooms with more than one exit may be safer.

9. The places I would try to avoid would be:

    _____

    _____

10. The places I would try to move to/stay in are:

_____

_____

11. In abusive situations, women sometimes say or do things that they would not in an equal non-abusive relationship. For some women, this involves survival skills such as claiming to agree with the abuser even when an accusation is not valid to increase safety. On other occasions, women may retaliate against the abuser with violence; however, be aware that such actions could lead you to be charged with a criminal offense.

12. Calling the police.

13. Given my past experience, other protective actions that I have considered or employed are:

_____

_____

_____

Safety Planning if you are Getting Ready to Leave

Some women leave the residence they share with the abusive partner. These are protective actions you may wish to consider if you are in this situation. Even if you are not planning to leave your partner, it is essential to review a safety plan regarding leaving if the violence escalates and you need to go quickly.

I can use the following strategies:

1. It may not be safe to inform my partner that I am leaving.

2. Should I need to leave quickly, it would be helpful for me to leave some extra cash, an extra set of house and car keys and extra clothes with some people who I can go to for help:_____

   _____

   and _____.

3. I can keep copies of important documents such as immigration papers or birth certificates at someone's house:_____

   _____.

4. I can open a savings account to increase my freedom to leave. I should make sure to alert the bank not to send any correspondence to my home address.

5. Other things I can do to increase my independence are:_____

   _____

6. The domestic violence hotline is _____

   _____.

   I can seek safe shelter and support by calling this helpline.

7. Telephone numbers I need to know:
   For safety reasons, it may be necessary to keep these telephone numbers hidden but accessible or memorize the numbers:

   Police Department:_____

Domestic Abuse Help Line (24 hours):_____

_____

Attorney:_____

Work:_____

Pastor: _____

Other:

_____

_____

_____

8. I can get legal advice from a victim advocate who understands domestic abuse. But as with the bank, I should make certain the advocate knows not to send any correspondence to my home address. It is critical to consult with a family advocate if you have children. Your local domestic abuse service may be able to recommend a suitable legal advocate.

9. I must be careful if I am using my mobile or home number because my partner or ex could see the numbers I have called on next month's telephone bill. I can keep telephone calls confidential using a burner phone, a prepaid phone card, a pay-as-you-go mobile phone, a friend's telephone card, or calling collect.

10. These are people that I could ask for assistance with: Money:_____

_____

_____

Child care:_____

_____

_____

Support-attending appointments:_____

_____

_____

_____

Transportation:

_____

_____

_____

Other:

_____

_____

_____

11. If I need to return home to get personal belongings, I can call the police for an escort to stand by and keep the peace. To do this, I call_____ (the non-emergency local police number) and ask the police to meet me somewhere close to my home. They will stay while I pick up my own and my children's personal belongings.

12. I will review my safety plan every_____ _____(time frame) in order to plan the safest route. I will review the plan with_____(a friend, counselor, or advocate).

13. I will rehearse the escape plan and practice it with my children.

14. When you leave an abusive partner, it is essential to take certain items with you. Items with asterisks on the following list are the most important, but the other items might be taken or stored outside the home if there is time. Keeping them all together in one location makes it much easier if you need to leave in a hurry.

- Identification for myself
- Children's birth certificates*
- Any papers relating to injunctions or other legal proceedings*
- My birth certificate*
- Immigration papers*
- School and vaccination records*
- Money*
- Checkbook, bankbook/cards*
- Credit Cards*
- Keys—house/car/office*
- Driver's license and car ownership details*
- Medications*
- Passport(s)*
- Any medical records*
- Divorce/separation papers*
- House lease/mortgage/insurance documents*
- Address book*
- Pictures/photos
- Children's favorite toys/blankets
- Jewelry
- Items of special sentimental value

15. Other protective actions I have considered are:

_____

_____

_____

_____

Safety in your Own Home

The following are some suggestions regarding safety measures in your own home that you may wish to consider (some of these safety measures cost money).

I can use the following safety methods:

1. If financially possible, I could:
    - Change the locks on my doors and windows as soon as possible. (You may need to inform the landlord if you are renting or consult legal counsel if you own your home before taking this action.)
    - Install a peephole in the door.
    - Replace wooden doors with steel doors.
    - Install security systems—i.e., additional locks, window bars, poles to wedge against doors, electronic alarm systems, etc.
    - Purchase rope ladders to be used for escape routes from the second floor.
    - Install smoke detectors and buy fire extinguishers for each floor of my home.
    - Install a motion-sensitive lighting system outside that lights up when a person is coming close to my home.
    - Leave the lights on at night and when I am away from home.

2. If I have custody, I can inform all the people who provide childcare for my children about who has permission to pick up my children and who does not. I can give these people copies of the custody order to keep with them and a picture of the abusive partner. I will tell the people who care for my children, who have permission to pick up my children. The people I will inform about pickup permission include:

School:

_____

Teacher:

_____

Day Care staff:_____

_____

Before/ After-School Care:_____

_____

Babysitter: _____

Sunday School:_____

Relatives: _____

Others: _____

3. I can teach my children how to use the phone to make 911 calls and how to call me or_____

_____

(friend, family, minister) if my partner tries to take them.

4. I can tell the following people that my partner no longer lives with me and ask that they should call the police if he is seen near my residence:

Neighbors_____

Landlord_____

Church Leaders_____

Friends_____

_____

Others_____

5. Other strategies that I am already using or that I might us include:

_____

_____

_____

_____

_____

_____

_____

Safety at Work and in Public

Each woman must decide if or when she will tell others that her partner has abused her and that she may be at continued risk. Friends. Family and coworkers may be able to help protect women. Each woman should carefully consider which people to recruit to help secure her safety. I might do any or all of the following:

1. If it is comfortable to do so, I can tell my boss, security, and _____at work about this situation.

2. According to how comfortable and safe I feel, I can ask _____to help screen my phone calls.

3. If it is comfortable to do so and support me and my situation, I could discuss the possibility of having my

employer call the police if I am in danger from my partner or ex.

4. Some safety suggestions regarding arriving or leaving work:
   - Let someone know when you'll be home
   - Walk with someone to your car
   - Scan the parking lot
   - If your partner is following you, drive to a place where there are people to support you, e.g., a friend's home, police station
   - If you are walking, take a route that is populated
   - Take different routes home
   - If you see your partner on the street, try to get to a public place
   - You can also call attention to yourself and request help
   - Purchase a personal alarm device

5. When I am driving home from work and problems arise, I can_____
   _____.

6. I can use different supermarkets/shopping centers and shop at other times than before to reduce the risk of contact with my partner or ex.

Safety and Drug or Alcohol Consumption

Alcohol and drugs are sometimes used as coping mechanisms for victims of domestic violence. The disclosure of the use of illegal/legal drugs can put a woman at a disadvantage in legal actions with her abusive partner.

Therefore, women should carefully consider the potential cost of using legal or illegal drugs. Beyond this, using any alcohol or other drugs can reduce a woman's awareness and ability to act quickly to protect herself from the abusive partner. Furthermore, the use of alcohol or other drugs by the abuser may be used as an excuse for violence.

Safety and Emotional Health

Being subjected to abuse by partners is usually exhausting and emotionally draining. The process of surviving requires much courage and incredible energy. To conserve my emotional energy and resources and to support myself in hard emotional times, I can do some of the following:

1. If I have left the relationship and I am experiencing loneliness or manipulative tactics from my abusive partner, I can take care of myself by:_____

   _____

   _____.

2. If I feel sad, lonely, or depressed and desire to return to a potentially violent situation/partner, I can

   _____

   and I can call _____.

3. When I have to talk to my partner in person or on the phone, I can emotionally prepare by_____

   _____

   _____

   _____

4. I can remind myself "_____
   _____"
   if I think people are trying to control or abuse me.

5. When I face potentially difficult times like court
   cases, meeting with lawyers and such, I can prepare
   by doing the following_____
   _____
   _____
   _____

6. I can call the following people and/or places for
   support: _____
   _____
   _____

7. Things I can do to make myself stronger are____
   _____
   _____
   _____

Appendix C

Beginning Framework-

Mediator Guidelines[91]

Overall goal – develop a framework of interaction to help two households function separately while each person is focusing on counseling and soul care.

Finances

Goal:

- Ensure adequate funds are allotted for each separate household to pay monthly bills and keep the two households functioning.
- Ensure that existing debts payments are kept current and do not enter default.

Method:

- Meet with each individually
- Gather overall assessment of current financial conditions (existing assets, existing debts)
- Access individual household monthly expenses and define monthly needs
- Access monthly income and compare to defined monthly needs (visit alternate arrangements if required)
- Allot money for separate monthly expenses
- Create a plan to keep current joint debt payments in place
- Create no future joint debts

---

[91] Beginning Framework originally created by Peter Hauff, 2018. Used by permission. Edited 2020.

Household
Goal:
- Develop two separately functioning households.

Method:
- Allocate appropriate funding for each – see finances above.
- Coordinate physical assistance as needed for daily tasks (mowing/septic/maintenance, etc.)

Children
Goal:
- Develop a framework for interactions, visits, custody.

Method:
- Seek input from all individuals involved (separately) to ensure clear communication between all parties.
- Develop a weekly calendar of visits/custody sharing
- Develop methods to communicate changes in the calendar.

Communication
Goal:
- Provide communication support, direction, and accountability between the parties specifically related to the above concerns.

Method:
- Email and text message communication can be relayed directly to the mediator for consideration and forwarding to the other as needed.
- No actions are to be taken by either party until discussed/approved by both parties and confirmed to be the mediator.
- The mediator will keep records of all communications.
- See **Mediator Communications** document

Appendix D

Mediator Communication[92]

Purpose:

The mediator's goal is to help facilitate daily functions and communications to enable the couple to work on counseling goals.

Scope:

The mediator will be the line of communication for relaying information, questions, or concerns between the parties regarding the following topics:

- Housing (maintenance, operations, automotive concerns)
- Financial (monthly budget, monthly bills, school expenses)
- Family event schedules (coordinating children's event attendance, ensuring weekly time with the children)
- Other questions regarding daily routines, household functions, etc.

Note: The children are not to act as the mediator or communicator between the two parents for any reason. We encourage the children to communicate with each parent

---

[92] Mediator Communication created by Peter Hauff, 2018. Used by permission.

individually, but children should not be asked to relay messages between their parents.

Not in scope of Mediator:

1. Spiritual Matters - The biblical counseling team (not the Mediator) is to be contacted for interpersonal concerns as the couple works and grows individually.

Methods:

1. Phone calls- home or cell phone. The Mediator is not always available; messages can be left on voicemail if desired.
   a. Home phone-
   b. Cell phone- (text messaging is also an option)

2. E-mail- This may be a more straightforward method to transfer multiple or lengthy messages.
   a. E-mail address-

Transmit information about another mediator who will also be assisting in this process. Contact details will be relayed when available.

Appendix E

Biblical Communication

I. The Importance of Communication

A. Communication Basics

1. Communication is necessary for relationships, and most people don't know how to communicate. James 3:2

a. Our speech is a powerful tool for either good or bad. Proverbs 18:21

b. Our speech impacts many other aspects of our lives. James 3:6

c. Communication is either honorable or dishonorable. Ephesians 4:29; Proverbs 15:2 Proverbs 12:18; Proverbs 18:21

d. Communication is either effective or ineffective. Proverbs 16:23; 2 Timothy 3:16; Matthew 5:37; Proverbs 17:27; Proverbs 27:17

II. Principles of Communication

A. Good communication begins with listening.

1. The poor listener. Proverbs 18:2

a. The poor listener is not listening to understand, nor are they engaged in the conversation.

b. The poor listener is quick to give advice or counsel. Proverbs 18:13, 13:3, 13:9

    c. A poor listener will not hear what you do say.

    d. The poor listener often argues.

2. The good listener.

    a. An attentive listener demonstrates patience and humility. Philippians 2:3

    b. Good listening requires attention. Proverbs 18:15

    c. The good listener seeks out and probes for accurate and adequate knowledge of what the other person is trying to communicate.

3. Put away lying. Ephesians 4:25

    a. Outright lies. Proverbs 12:22, 6:16-17; Psalm 120:2

    b. Exaggerate or embellish the story - Adding details to the story that make it better or worse than it really was.

    c. Manipulating the facts to make yourself look better.

    d. Subtle lies.

    e. Mixing truth with lies.

4. Speak the truth.

    a. Speak the truth compassionately.

    b. Speak the truth directly to those who need to hear it. Proverbs 18:17

    c. Speak the truth with grace. Colossians 4:6

5. Stay in the day. Ephesians 4:26-27

6. Get angry, but do not sin.

a. Not all anger is sinful; God gets angry. Psalm 7:11; 2 Kings 17:16-18; Zechariah 1:2-6; Hebrews 3:7-11; Mark 3:5

7. Righteous anger is over sins against God.

8. Anger that does not have to do with God's righteous standards is not righteous anger.

   a. Anger can be dangerous. Matthew 5:22

   b. Anger is sinful when it is used to attack people (venting).

   c. Anger is sinful when it is stuffed and held inside without resolution (clamming up). Proverbs 25:28; Ephesians 4:26-27

   d. Solve today's problems today. Matthew 6:34; Ephesians 4:26

   e. Don't let the sun go down on your anger.

   f. When anger is not addressed biblically, it becomes bitterness. Hebrews 12:15

9. Attack the problem, not the person.

   a. Don't let "garbage talk" come out of your mouths. Ephesians 4:29

      1) "Unwholesome words" = Sapros – corrupt or foul, often used for rotten fruit, vegetables, or other spoiled food.

      2) Words that attack a person's character. Matthew 5:21-22

      3) Words that burn and destroy a person. James 3:8

      4) Destructive, judgmental words. Psalm 52:2; Proverbs 12:18

5) Words that complicate the issue.

6) Words that grieve the Holy Spirit. Ephesians 4:30

10. Use "edifying" communication that gives grace to the hearer. Ephesians 4:15, 29

a. Use words that address the problem.

b. Speak the truth in love and to solve the problem.

c. Use words that are helpful, build up.

d. Use words that are other-oriented.

e. Use words that are aimed at solving problems, not to win an argument.

11. Don't react. Ephesians 4:31–32

a. Reactions, attitudes, and actions that must be "put off." v. 31

b. Actions and attitudes that must be "put on." v. 32

c. You, through God's Spirit, must learn to be kind, tenderhearted

Appendix F

Additional Counseling Issues

Below you will find some additional counseling issues that may be present in either the husband or the wife. These sin problems are listed in the following Scriptures: 1 Timothy 6:4-5; Ephesians 4:29-30; Galatians 5:19-21; 2 Timothy 3:8; Colossians 3:6; Matthew 7; 2 Peter 3:16; Psalm 56:5; 1 Corinthians 13:13 (opposite of)

Backbiting
Bitterness
Blame-shifting
Blaspheming
Brawling
Brutality
Conceit
Cursing/filthy language
Deception/lies
Deceitful desires/lust
Envy
Evil suspicion
Faithlessness
Fits of rage
Foolishness
Greed

Hopelessness
Jealousy
Lack of self-control
Lovelessness
Loves evil
Loves pleasure
Malice
Manipulative
Murderous
Pride
Obsession with disputes and arguments over words
Rage
Rashness
Rebellion

Scheming
Selfishness
Self-control
Self-righteousness
Self-serving
Sexually immoral
Slanderous
Strife
Treacherous
Under-serving
Unforgiving
Ungrateful
Unholy
Unloving
Unmerciful
Wickedness

Appendix G

Full Disclosure

This document can be used as a guide to help a counselee to prepare their full disclosure. Regarding the use of the word "ever" in the form, we intentionally use this word because abusers tend to minimize and rationalize their actions. The counselors will want to ask clarifying questions to determine the frequency or intensity of the statements.

1. Have you ever: (Circle all that apply)
    a. Physically harmed or physically frightened your wife
    b. Slapped her
    c. Punched her
    d. Grabbed her arm or neck roughly
    e. Raised a hand or fist to her
    f. Kicked her
    g. Shoved her
    h. Thrown something at her
    i. Tore her clothes
    j. Pulled her hair
    k. Spit at her
    l. Restrained her
    m. Other _____

2. Have you ever: (Circle all that apply)
    a. Frightened your wife by using certain looks, gestures, or actions?
    b. Screamed at her (when alone or in front of the children)
    c. Act without warning from kind to cruel or explosive
    d. Broken things in front of her

e. Destroyed her property
f. Displayed weapons
g. Threatened to kill your wife or yourself in front of her
h. Other _____

3. Have you ever been: (Circle all that apply)
    a. Accused of being abusive
    b. Accused of displaying abusive behaviors

4. How have you responded to the accusations:
    a. Made light of the abuse
    b. Rationalized your behavior
    c. Justified your behavior
    d. Said it was her fault
    e. Said it did not happen
    f. Blamed your wife or someone else for your failures or frustrations
    g. Acted remorseful after being angry, then withdraw and tensions build

5. Have you ever: (Circle all that apply)
    a. Ridiculed your wife?
    b. Put her down
    c. Called her names
    d. Humiliated her in person or in front of others
    e. Made her feel guilty
    f. Belittled your wife's accomplishments
    g. Punish her with long silences
    h. Interrupted her sleep or her eating
    i. Accused her of flirting or cheating on you
    j. Attempted to catch your wife in a wrong

6. Have you ever: (Circle all that apply)

a. Kept her from going places (Work, school, seeing family or friends, store)
b. Opened her mail
c. Listened in on phone conversations
d. Threatened to teach her a lesson
e. Followed her: (in the car, room to room)
f. Resented the time she spends with family and friends
g. Blocked her: (from leaving home or moving from room to room)
h. Questioned her about her whereabouts

7. Have you ever: Circle all that apply)
a. Told the children she is not a good mother
b. Threatened to take away the children
c. Used the children to relay messages
d. Used visitation to harass her
e. Used visitation to have sexual relations with you
f. Taken advantage of your wife sexually

8. Have you ever: (Circle all that apply)
a. Treated her like a servant
b. Acted like the master of the castle
c. Told her what her role or job was
d. Avoided doing your fair share of the housework
e. Made household rules without her input
f. Expected her to be sexual when you wanted
g. Other_____

9. Have you ever: (Circle all that apply)
a. Prevented her from working outside the home
b. Made her ask for money
c. Kept the finances to yourself even when asked for information

d. Withheld information on the family income
e. Kept the checkbook from her
f. Made major financial decisions without her input
g. Made expensive purchases without her input
h. Not paid child support

10. Have you ever: (Circle all that apply)
    a. Made threats to leave her
    b. Made threats to take the children
    c. Made threats to divorce her
    d. Threatened to harm her
    e. Threatened to harm her family members or friends
    f. Threatened suicide
    g. Made her do illegal things

11. Have you ever: (Circle all that apply)
    a. Used scriptures to support any of the above behaviors
    b. Used scriptures to demand her submission
    c. Used scriptures to ridicule, demean, judge, or condemn her
    d. Used scriptures to require her to forgive you
    e. Used scriptures to excuse your behavior
    f. Used scriptures to make her feel guilty

Appendix H

Victim Impact Statement

Use this outline to help you write a statement of how you have been harmed and affected by the abuse you have suffered at the hands of your spouse. Be thorough and detailed. You will have an opportunity to read this to your spouse in a special counseling session.

- Outline each of the physical, emotional, verbal, sexual, and spiritual abuse incidents you can recall in as much detail as you can remember.
- Tell your spouse the physical, emotional, verbal, sexual, and spiritual impacts each abuse incident had on you.
- Tell your spouse how you felt while being abused and the effects the abuse had on how you responded to your husband/wife throughout the marriage.
- Tell your spouse how the abuse affected the children and the extended family.
- Tell your spouse how the abuse affected your job or career.
- Include how you have been changed because of the abuse.
- Include how you have been changed because of biblical counseling.
- What you have learned about abuse.
- What you have learned about yourself.
- How you will never allow things to go back to the way they were.

Bibliography

Dryburgh, A. (n.d.). *Debilitated and Diminished: Help for Christian Women in Emotionally Abusive Marriages.* Self Published.

Farlex. "Abusing." *The Free Dictionary* 2019. https://www.thefreedictionary.com/abusing

Fitzpatrick, E. (2008). *Because He Loves Me: How Christ Transforms Our Daily Life.* Wheaton: Crossway books.

_____ (2003). *Helper by Design.* Chicago: Moody Publishers.

Forrest, J. (2018). *Called to Peace: a survivor's guide to finding Peace and Healing after Domestic Abuse.* Raleigh: Blue Ink Press.

Ganschow, J. & Roeder, B. (2013). *The Process of Biblical Heart Change.* Kansas City: Pure Water Press.

Ganschow, J. (2009). *The Process of Biblical Change.* Kansas City: Pure Water Press.

Grudem, W. (1994) *Systematic Theology: An Introduction to Biblical Doctrine.* Grand Rapids: Zondervan.

Hambrick, B. (2014). *Self-Centered Spouse: Help for Chronically Broken Marriages .* Phillipsburg: P & R Publishing Company.

Hauff, P. (2018). Beginning Framework.

Holcomb, J. and Holcomb, L. (2014). *Is It My Fault? Hope and Healing for Those Suffering Domestic Violence, .* Chicago: Moody Publishers.

Kellemen, R. W. (2013). *Sexual Abuse - Beauty for Ashes.* Phillipsburg: P&R Publishing Company.

MacArthur, J. (2005). *The MacArthur Bible Commentary.* Nashville: Thomas Nelson.

Moles, C. (2015). *The Heart of Domestic Abuse: Gospel Solutions for Men Who Use Control and Violence in the Home.* Bemidji: Focus Publishing.

National Domestic Violence Hotline, General, https://www.thehotline.org/resources/statistics/,

Packer, J.I., (1982). *Daily Life in Bible Times,* Ed. James I Packer, Merrill C. Tenney, William White, Jr. (Nashville: Thomas Nelson Publishers.

Peace, M. (1998). *The Excellent Wife.* Bemidji: Focus Publishing.

Powlison, D. (2008). Recovering from Child Abuse, Greensboro: New Growth Press; 1st edition.

_____(2014) *I'll Never Get Over it: Help for the Aggrieved.* The Journal of Biblical Counseling 28:1, 8-27. Glenside: Christian Counseling & Educational Foundation.

Pryde, D. and Needham, R. (2003). *A Biblical Perspective of What to do When You Are Abused by Your Husband.* Newberry Springs: Iron Sharpeneth Iron Publications.

Scott, S. (2002). *The Exemplary Husband.* Bemidji: Focus Publishing.

Somerville, R. *Dealing With Anger Completely!* Retrieved from bobs@vefc.net: https://biblicalcounseling.com/store/all-products/dealing-with-anger-in-a-godly-way-bob-somerville-breakout-session-1/

Taylor, J. (2015, April 25). *Hyper-Headship and the Scandal of Domestic Abuse in the Church.* Retrieved from The Gospel Coalition: https://www.thegospelcoalition.org/blogs/justin-taylor/hyper-headship-and-the-scandal-of-domestic-abuse-in-the-church/

Thomas, R. (2016, August 28). *emotional-abuse-its-origins-its-cure*. Retrieved from www.rickthomas.net: www.rickthomas.net/emotional-abuse-its-origins-its-cure/

_____ *Can a Christian Divorce Another Christian For Abuse?* Retrieved from rickthomas.net: https://rickthomas.net/can-a-christian-divorce-another-christian-for-abuse/

Tripp, P. (2002). *Instruments in the Redeemers Hands.* P&R Publishing, Glenside.

About The Authors

Julie Ganschow, Ph.D. is the founder and Director of Reigning Grace Counseling Center and Biblical Counseling for Women. She is certified with the Association of Certified Biblical Counselors (ACBC) and the International Association of Biblical Counselors (IABC). Julie serves on the advisory board of The Fallen Soldiers March (FSM), and is a Commissioned Biblical Counselor (CBC) with The Addiction Connection.

Julie has been involved in Biblical Counseling and Discipleship for more than 25 years. Julie is a gifted counselor and teacher, a frequent retreat and conference speaker, and a featured contributor in GriefShare. She is the author of numerous books, articles, and materials for biblical counseling and has co-authored a biblical counseling training course.

She makes her home in Kansas City, Missouri with her wonderful husband Larry. They have three children and 2 grandchildren.

Bill Schlacks began his career as a licensed counselor working as a mental health counselor seeing individual, couples, and families. He was frustrated by the use of medication for symptom relief and the lack of change in the lives of his counselees. God graciously redeemed him and Bill left the mental health system. He received his certification as an IABC biblical counselor and has worked as a biblical counselor for nearly 30 years.

He is now seeing heart change and lives changed as his counselees apply the Word of God to their lives. Bill is on staff at Reigning Grace Counseling Center in Kansas City, Missouri.

He is married to his lovely wife, Susan. They have three children and three beautiful grandchildren.

OTHER BOOKS BY JULIE GANSCHOW

The Process of Biblical Change

The Process of Biblical Heart Change (workbook)with Bruce Roeder

A Biblical Perspective on Self-Injury

Questions on the Heart Level: Effective Question Asking for Biblical Counselors

Seeing Depression Through the Eyes of Grace

Living Beyond the Heart of Betrayal

You can find her blog at bc4women.org and information about her ministries at rgcconline.org, and biblicacounselingforwomen.org

www.ingramcontent.com/pod-product-compliance
Lightning Source LLC
Chambersburg PA
CBHW051821090426
42736CB00011B/1585